TWAYNE'S WORLD AUTHORS SERIES

A Survey of the World's Literature

Sylvia E. Bowman, Indiana University

GENERAL EDITOR

INDIA

M. L. Sharma, Slippery Rock State College

EDITOR

Jawaharlal Nehru

TWAS 345

Photo courtesy of Lotte Meitner-Graf, London

Jawaharlal Nehru

Jawaharlal Nehru

JOHN B. ALPHONSO-KARKALA

State University of New York at New Paltz

TWAYNE PUBLISHERS

A DIVISION OF G. K. HALL & CO., BOSTON

Library of Congress Cataloging in Publication Data

Alphonso-Karkala, John B   1923–
   Jawaharlal Nehru.

   (Twayne's world authors series; TWAS 345: India)
   Bibliography: p. 151–57.
   Includes index.
   1. Nehru, Jawaharlal, 1889–1964.

DS481.N35A74   954.04′092′4 [B]   74–20702

ISBN 0–8057–2649–7

To My Father
S. Anthony Apons

Contents

About the Author

John B. Alphonso-Karkala is Professor of Literature at the State University of New York at New Paltz, where he has been teaching Comparative and Asian Literature since 1964. He has also taught Oriental Humanities at Columbia University in New York. Prior to teaching, he served in the Indian Foreign Missions at Geneva, London, and at the United Nations in New York.

Dr. Alphonso-Karkala was born in South Kanara, Karnataka State, India. During his school days he participated in the Satyagraha movement as a Congress volunteer. After his early schooling in his hometown, he was educated at the Bombay University, London University, and Columbia University, majoring in Literature and Philosophy. He has pioneered research and teaching in Comparative Asian Literature studies. His papers presented at the congresses of international learned societies include "World Humanities in Undergraduate Education," (Bombay, 1965); "The Beginning of the Asian Novel," (Tokyo, 1966); "The Theme of Love and the use of poetic imagery in *Song of Solomon* and *Gita Govinda*," (Bordeaux, France, 1970); "Woman as Man's Resurrection in *Kalevala* and *Mahabharata*," (Chapel Hill, North Carolina, 1972); "Prospects for Comparative World Literature," (Saratoga Spring, NY, 1972); and "Transmission of Knowledge by Antero Vipunen to Väinämöinen in *Kalevala* and by Sukra to Kacha in *Mahabharata*," (Ottawa, Canada, 1973). His books are: *Indo-English Literature in the Nineteenth Century* (Mysore, 1970); *An Anthology of Indian Literature*: Vedas to Gitanjali (London & New York: Penguin, 1972); *Passions of Nightless Nights*, fiction (New Delhi, 1974); *Bibliography of Indo-English Literature: 1800–1966* (Bombay, 1974), and *Studies in Comparative World Literature* (Bombay, 1974). He is presently engaged in research and writing on a comparative approach to South Asian Literature.

Preface

JAWAHARLAL Nehru is well known as one of India's foremost freedom fighters, and after independence, as its Prime Minister and a world statesman from 1947 to 1964. His public life and his thoughts and ideas after he became the Prime Minister of India have been studied and discussed in many books. What is less known about him is that while he was struggling with the freedom movement from 1913 to 1946, he also wrote in English a dozen books which rank him as a writer among world authors.

Jawaharlal's writings may be regarded as his contribution to modern Indian literature expressed in about seventeen languages, including Indo-English. Yet on account of his wide culture, unconventional world view, and extraordinary personality, his writings containing his thoughts and reflections on events in India and the world, place him among the molders of world opinion in this century.

Jawaharlal was an unusual man. The vicissitudes of his eventful life during the course of India's history provided him with many rare opportunities to observe the human condition from unique points of view. A person who could claim ancestry from India's cultural aristocracy, who had the best of education England could provide, who dreamed of "brave deeds with sword in hand" for India's freedom, who thought like a revolutionary and became a disciplined Satyagrahi under Gandhi's leadership, who in spite of being an intellectual and an internationalist became the idol of the illiterate village masses and youth, who voluntarily suffered nine imprisonments to redeem his oppressors—such a man, no doubt, has a rich store of experiences. As a practical politician he translated his thoughts into action whenever he had the opportunity to do so; but when that opportunity was denied to him by imprisonment, he set himself to the heroic task of translating his thoughts and visions into books, without bitterness or Swiftean satire. It is this crowded experience of an intense life of a man of refined sensibilities, unitary world view, with firm commitment to freedom and democracy, seeking social justice under humane conditions, that lifts the personality of the author from the local and national levels to the larger family of world authors.

The purpose of this study is to examine some of the significant influences in Jawaharlal's life which contributed to the making of a writer, and to discuss his works. A brief sketch of his formative years is provided in the introductory chapter, giving some accounts of his childhood and youth, English education, his involvement in the national movement, his apprenticeship in international politics in Europe, his contacts with progressive and liberal thinkers of his time, and the circumstances during the long freedom struggle which led him to write his books. In the succeeding chapters, Jawaharlal's occasional writings and major works are discussed.

I am grateful to Mrs. Indira Gandhi, the Prime Minister of India, and the officials of Jawaharlal Nehru Museum at New Delhi for their kind help and cooperation. Also, I am grateful to the Research Foundation of the State University of New York, Albany, N.Y., for the support given in the form of research fellowships and grant. I want to express my indebtedness to my wife, Leena, without whose continous help and assistance this manuscript would not have been completed.

JOHN B. ALPHONSO-KARKALA

State University of New York at New Paltz

Acknowledgments

I am grateful for permissions granted to quote from the copyrighted editions of Jawaharlal Nehru's works, to the following:

Mrs. Indira Gandhi, Prime Minister of India, and Jawaharlal Nehru Estate for quotations from *Soviet Russian, Letters from a Father to His Daughter*, and *The Unity of India*.

Kitabistan, Allahabad, for quotations from *Recent Essays and Writings*, and *Eighteen Months in India*.

Asia Publishing House, Bombay, for quotations from *Glimpses of World History*, and *The Discovery of India*.

University and National Book Suppliers, Allahabad, for quotations from *Pandit Jawaharlal Nehru: Statements, Speeches and Writings*.

John Lane, The Bodley Head Ltd., London, and Allied Publishers Private Lt., Bombay, for quotations from *An Autobiography*; and John Day Co. Inc., New York, for quotations from *Toward Freedom: The Autobiography of Jawaharlal Nehru*.

Chronology

1889   Born in Allahabad, Nov.14, son of Motilal and Swarup-rani; early education by private tutors.

1905–   Studied in England at Harrow, Cambridge, and Inner
1912   Temple.

1912   Delegate to the Indian National Congress.

1915   Gandhi returned to India from South Africa.

1916   Married Kamala Kaul in Delhi, Feb. 8; met Gandhi at Congress session.

1917   Daughter Indira born in Allahabad, Nov. 19.

1919   Jallianwala Bagh massacre; appointed Deputy to the Inquiry Committee.

1920   With Gandhi met Rabindranath Tagore in Santiniketan.

1921   Gandhi launched Non-Cooperation Movement; imprisoned (I), 87 days.

1922–   Imprisoned (II), 265 days; "Statement in the Court."
1923

1923   Mayor of Allahabad, resigned 1925; imprisoned (III), 12 days; "Statement in the Court"; President, U.P. Provincial Congress.

1924   Secretary, All-India Congress Committee; resigned 1926.

1926–   In Europe 21 months: Kamala taken for treatment; par-
1927   ticipated in Brussels Congress of the Oppressed, Feb. 27, and in the Tenth Jubilee Anniversary of Soviet Revolution in Moscow, Nov. 27.

1927   Moved Complete Independence Resolution at Congress session.

1928   General Secretary of the Congress; wrote letters to Indira; *Soviet Russia.*

1929   President of the Congress; *Statements, Speeches, and Writings.*

1930	Gandhi launched Salt Satyagraha; imprisoned (IV), 180 days; *Letters from a Father to His Daughter.*
1930– 1931	Imprisoned (V), 99 days; wrote further letters to Indira, nn. 1–18.
1931	Motilal died, Feb. 6; visited Ceylon; wrote further letters, nn. 19–20.
1931– 1933	Imprisoned (VI), 612 days; wrote further letters, nn. 21–196.
1933	*Whither India?*
1934	*Recent Essays and Writings*; *Glimpses of World History.*
1934– 1935	Imprisoned (VII), 569 days; wrote autobiography.
1935	Kamala critically ill, taken by friends to Germany in May; upon release rushed to Europe in Sept.
1936	Kamala died in Lausanne, Switzerland, Feb. 28; President of the Congress; *An Autobiography*; *India and the World.*
1937	Visited Burma and Malaya.
1938	Visited Europe: England, Spain, and Czechoslovakia; *Eighteen Months in India.*
1939	Visited Ceylon and China; war declared in Europe.
1940	*China, Spain, and the War.*
1940– 1942	Imprisoned (VIII), 398 days; "Statement in the Court"; *The Unity of India*, ed. V.K. Krishna Menon.
1941	Tagore died, Aug. 7.
1942	Gandhi moved Quit India Resolution in the Congress.
1942– 1945	Imprisoned (IX), 1,040 days; wrote *The Discovery of India.*
1945	Participated in the Simla Conference on the transfer of power.
1946	*The Discovery of India.*
1946– 1947	Prime Minister, Government of India (Interim), eleven months.
1947	India declared independent, Aug. 15; Pakistan created.
1947– 1950	Prime Minister, Government of India (Independent), two years, five months.
1948	Gandhi assassinated in Delhi, Jan. 30.
1950	India declared a Republic, Jan. 26.
1950– 1964	Prime Minister, Government of India (Republic), fourteen years, four months.
1964	Died in Delhi, May 27, at the age of 74.

CHAPTER 1

Jawaharlal Nehru: A Brief Sketch

I Childhood and Youth, 1889–1905

JAWAHARLAL, the first child and the only son of Motilal Nehru
and Swarup-rani was born in the ancient city of Prayag (or Allahabad), situated at the confluence of the sacred rivers, the Ganges
and the Jamna. Motilal was a prosperous lawyer and a prominent
member of the Indian National Congress. Besides claiming descent
from a Kashmiri Brahmin family, Motilal had added to his aristocratic household many doses of European ways of life. He was "fond
of good living in every way."[1]

Jawaharlal grew up in a larger joint-family household, consisting
of older cousins and near relatives; yet he spent his childhood as a
somewhat "lonely child with no companions" of his own age either
at home or at school. For he was privately educated by tutors at
home. His sisters, Vijayalakshmi (married to Ranjit Pundit), was
born eleven years later in 1900, and Krishna (married to Raja
Hutheesing), seven years thereafter in 1907. During most of his early
years, Jawaharlal was left a great deal to his own "fancies and solitary games."

As a young boy, Jawaharlal much admired his father and his ways
of gay life, laughter, and free association with Englishmen; but he
also feared him when he lost his temper at servants and others. On
the other hand, he grew fond of his mother who, he felt, would con-
done him everything.

Because of the English governesses and tutors at home, and foreign friends who visited them, the Nehru family had developed warm
feelings for individual Europeans. In spite of these associations,
Jawaharlal recalls, "quarrels took place, especially during railway
journeys," among his relatives and the English or Eurasian officials,

1

mainly because of the arrogance and offensive behavior of the latter, and their claim for undue privileges.

During his early years, Jawaharlal was exposed to a cosmopolitan culture. While the English governesses provided him with European orientation, Jawaharlal's mother and aunt gave him the basic exposure to the roots of Indian culture, through the familiar art of storytelling. With the oral transmission of the ancient wisdom contained in the Indian classics, especially the *Ramayana*, the *Mahabharata*, the *Puranas*, and the *Panchatantra*, Jawaharlal claims, his knowledge of the tradition grew considerably. There was also his father's *munshi* (or clerk), Mubarak Ali, an elderly bearded man, whose family was exterminated by the English troops. Ali related to the child his memories of the national uprising in 1857, and many stories from the *Arabian Nights.*

In his youth, Jawaharlal participated in many of the religious ceremonies, such as *pujas*, dips in the Ganges, visits to Sanyasis and holy men. Yet as he grew up, he says, he tried to imitate the casual attitude of the grown-up men in the family, namely regarding religion "to be a woman's affair." He particularly enjoyed playing pranks during some of the national festivals and at the marriage parties, which were great occasions for the family reunion when he had the company of other children.

In 1899 Motilal moved his family to a new and bigger house named "Anand Bhawan," a place destined to achieve historical importance. Here Jawaharlal saw his sheltered and uneventful life change in many ways. When his father returned from a visit to England, there was a great commotion in the house as he challenged the orthodox Kashmiri Brahmin community by refusing to go through a purification ceremony which was a bit of a farce; yet within two years, Motilal arranged for the *Upanayana* (or twice-born sacred thread) ceremony for his son at the age of twelve. The following year, Motilal allowed his son to be initiated into Theosophy by the high-priestess, Mrs. Annie Beasant. Jawaharlal recalls that during those two years he "developed the flat and insipid look which sometimes denotes piety."[2] A learned Pundit regularly came to the house to spend his best efforts in teaching young Jawaharlal Hindi and Sanskrit. But a more radical change came with the arrival of a new resident tutor, Ferdinand T. Brooks, who, taking charge of the young boy, introduced him to the proper mysteries of "English Education." Besides spending long hours in a rigged up little laboratory in the house, Jawaharlal also developed a taste for reading:

I read a great many English books, though rather aimlessly. I was well up in children's and boys' literature; the Lewis Carroll books were great favorites, and *The Jungle Books* and *Kim*. I was fascinated by Gustave Dore's illustrations to *Don Quixote*, and Fridtjof Nansen's *Farthest North* opened out a new realm of adventure to me. I remember reading many of the novels of Scott, Dickens and Thackeray, H. G. Wells' romances, Mark Twain, and Sherlock Holmes stories. I was thrilled by the *Prisoner of Zenda*, and Jerome K. Jerome's *Three Men in a Boat* was for me the last word in humor. Another book stands out still in my memory; it was Du Maurier's *Trilby*, also *Peter Ibbetson*. I also developed a liking for poetry, a liking which has to some extent endured and survived the many other changes to which I have been subject.[3]

In a house visited by nationalist leaders and foreign guests, the international topics were often centers of heated discussions. The newspapers were then full of headlines of current world events. As a boy, Jawaharlal was deeply influenced by them and the two wars: first, England's Boer War of 1889–1901 in Africa, and the second, which had a profounder effect, the Russo–Japanese War of 1904. Newspaper accounts of these wars, especially Japanese victories, stirred in him heroic enthusiasm: "Nationalistic ideas filled my mind. I mused of Indian freedom and Asiatic freedom from the thraldom of Europe. I dreamt of brave deeds, of how, sword in hand, I would fight for India and help in freeing her."[4] As a result he "invested in a large number of books on Japan", studied Japanese history, and enjoyed reading "the knightly tales of old Japan and the pleasant prose of Lafcadio Hearn."

Thus before leaving for England in 1905, Jawaharlal had already come to sense in some vague way the need for a heroic struggle to liberate India from the British domination.

II *English Education, 1905–1912*

Jawaharlal spent seven years in England, attending a prestigious public school at Harrow (1905–07), pursuing studies in Science at Trinity College of Cambridge University (1907–10), and studying law at the Inner Temple, London (1910–12). During this period of intellectual sophistication, Jawaharlal became acquainted, in the

British institutions and society, with many aspects of European ideologies, liberal ideals, scientific methodologies, independence of
thought, and modern approaches to life and its problems.

The public school at Harrow, about eleven miles to the northwest
of London, established in 1572 as a parish school, admitted many
"foreigners," meaning students from other English parishes; but in
later years students from other countries were also admitted. It was
a training ground for many outstanding men. Two of its graduates
who were contemporaries, and who subsequently becoming heads of
government confronted each other on the question of the dissolution
of the British Empire were Winston Churchill and Jawaharlal Nehru.

Jawaharlal found the school a totally new world and was home-
sick for a while. But he soon got used to the work and took full share
of his studies and games. He found the English boys most dull as
"they could talk about nothing but their games." There was considerable anti-Semitic feeling towards Jewish boys even though they
were able to get along with others.[5] Though Jawaharlal developed
a new interest in aviation, his greater involvement remained with
public affairs and international events. When a new government was
formed in London, he was the only boy in his class who could give his
teacher almost a "complete list of members of Campbell–Banner-
man's Cabinet" to the annoyance of the English boys!

Even while he was away from home, Jawaharlal was emotionally
involved with national events in India. He was greatly agitated by the
volatile Arabindo Ghose (later Shri Aurobindo), who deprecating
the insipid Congress demand for reform within the colonial rule, was
urging national patriotism to purify and set free a decadent nation
through fire and blood sacrifice. For their freedom demand when
the Indian leaders like Lala Lajpat Rai, Ajit Singh, and Tilak were
tried for sedition and imprisoned or deported from their own home
land, Jawaharlal was deeply disturbed, but "there was not a soul in
Harrow" to whom he could talk about it.

When Jawaharlal left Harrow, he was given one volume of G. M.
Trevelyan's book *Garibaldi* as a prize for good work. On reading
this, he was so taken by Garibaldi's patriotic passion that he pur-
chased the other two volumes himself and read the whole Garibaldi
story and was fascinated by the national struggle in Italy. "Visions
of similar deeds in India," wrote Jawaharlal, "came before me, of a
gallant fight for freedom."[6]

Jawaharlal spent three years in Cambridge, taking natural sciences tripos (his subjects being chemistry, geology, and botany), and grad- uated with second class honors. In spite of this specialization he did not become a scientist or a narrow specialist. That was partly because during those quiet years, Jawaharlal becoming mentally alert, ab- sorbed current thoughts and speculations on a wide variety of hu- manities, and developed, so to say, "a kind of scientific humanism," neither exclusively tradition-bound, nor completely science dictated, but a synthesis of the two cultures. It was this scientific humanism with which he tried to experiment later in the national reconstruction of India, politically, economically, and culturally.

Jawaharlal's humanism developed during his academic and social life at Cambridge and London against the background of the general intellectual ferment in Europe. He met people talking "learnedly about books and literature and history and politics and economics," though in their highbrow company he often felt "a little at sea at first." But he read books and caught up with the general trend. "So we discussed Nietzsche (he was all the rage in Cambridge then) and Bernard Shaw's prefaces and the latest book by Lowes Dickinson. We considered ourselves very sophisticated and talked of sex and morality in a superior way, referring casually to Ivan Block, Have- lock Ellis, Kraft-Ebbing or Otto Weininger."[7] Another book which influenced him at this time was Meredith Townsend's *Asia and Europe.* Yet when it came to speaking at the Cambridge Debating Society, Jawaharlal was too shy, and often paid fines for "not speak- ing for a whole term."

Jawaharlal's unique achievement in Cambridge apparently was intangible. He claimed he was "moderately successful" since there were none of those academic distinctions to crown his college days. Yet in the quiet background of his mind he was debating within him- self, synthesizing his educational experiences and developing "a general attitude to life." First he found Edwin Montagu's modern definition of faith as being very practical and agreeable: faith is "to believe in something which your reason tells you cannot be true, for if your reason approved of it, there could be no question of blind faith"[8]; second, the revival of Renaissance sensibilities spearheaded by gurus like Walter Pater and later by Oscar Wilde fascinated him. The young Englishmen, basking in the material glory of the empire and caught in the mental agony of the tyrannizing concept of sin, were looking for "more wine and madder music" in the spirit of the fin de siècle, to enjoy soft life under the high-sounding philosophy of Cyrenaicism. To Jawaharlal, idealistically hoping to see political liberation and cultural revival in India, the decadent attitude did not fit in at all, but the "soft life" with slightly different emphasis attracted him. "Not having the religious temper and disliking the repressions of religion," he wrote, "it was natural for me to seek some other standard. . . . And so the aesthetic side of life appealed to me, and the idea . . . of going through life worthily, not indulging it in the vulgar way, but still making the most of it and living a full and many-sided life attracted me. I enjoyed life and I refused to see why I should consider it a thing of sin. At the same time risk and adventure fascinated me; I was always, like my father, a bit of a gambler, at first with money and then for higher stakes, with the bigger issues of life."[9]

Because of the gradual development of these attitudes to life, Jawaharlal was able to take great risks in bold adventures and gambles in India's progress from a colony to an independent nation and a significant member in the world community. Yet the aristocratic temper, the Renaissance gentlemanliness, and healthy paganism survived in Jawaharlal even in his later days in such grandiose mannerisms as the "chacha-Nehru" smile and the red rose in his buttonhole.

By the time Jawaharlal graduated from Cambridge, a decision had already been made that he should not join the British Indian civil service, but follow the "paternal profession, the bar." At the Inner Temple he studied law and got through the bar examinations "one after another, with neither glory nor ignominy." He was finally called to the bar in the summer of 1912.

During his seven-year stay in England, Jawaharlal visited India twice. He also visited Europe during the holidays, including Germany, France, Ireland, and Scandinavia. He was attracted by the way of life in Scandinavia, and by the aspirations of the Irish people. It was easy for him to identify himself with the Sinn Fein nationalists who were seeking to liberate their ancient country, in a "seven-hundred-year-long freedom struggle" from the common enemy, the imperial English government!

In the Fall of 1912 Jawaharlal returned to India with the best of education England could give. Yet as he landed in Bombay, he modestly and jokingly recalled that he felt "a bit of a prig with little to command."[10] Such a capacity for self-criticism was seldom found among English-educated stiff-necked Indians, who were more concerned about keeping the starch on their white collars and wearing the halo of "England-returned" status around them than about a critical self-examination.

III *Congress Worker, 1912–1925*

A. *Attorney-at-Law.* Upon his return to India, Jawaharlal joined the Allahabad High Court at the age of twenty-three and took up law practice. At that time he found India was "politically dull." When the Indian National Congress held its annual session at Banki-pur in Bihar in December, 1912, Jawaharlal attended as a delegate. It was essentially "an English-knowing upper-class affair where morning coats and well pressed trousers were greatly in evidence . . . a social gathering with no political excitement."[11] While the nation-alists were either kept in prison or exiled, the Congress was domi-nated by the so-called Moderates (that is, English-educated Indians with British sensibilities) who having shelved the question of Indian independence, were "passing feeble resolutions" in response to the British tune called out by Minto-Morley reforms. Macaulay's magic formula to keep the British Empire sustained on the Indian fifth col-umn was exercising its charm successfully.

World War I somewhat changed the political scene in India. Promising vague self-rule to India after the war, British government forcibly pressed many able-bodied Indians into the British army to fight a war primarily meant to protect and preserve British Empire and its economic interests in the name of "freedom and democracy" while at the same time denying that very freedom to India. About this time, M. K. Gandhi, leaving his South African experiments be-hind arrived in Bombay on January 9, 1915. His work had stirred the imagination of men of goodwill throughout the world. Yet on his return to India, Gandhi kept away from the Congress politics, and toured the country for a year.

On February 8, 1916, Jawaharlal married Kamala Kaul, daughter of a Kashmiri family in Delhi. Thereafter the Nehru family visited Kashmir for holidays; Jawaharlal went up the mountains alone and spent several weeks communing with the Himalayan peaks.

That same year Tilak and Mrs. Annie Beasant, leader of the The-osophical Movement in India, founded the Home Rule League, demanding self-government for India, but the British government responded by imprisoning them both. When the Congress held its session in December in Lucknow, Jawaharlal met Gandhi for the first time. Then both men were somewhat nonentities in Congress politics. Listening to poetess Sarojini Naidu's eloquent, lyrical, and patriotic speeches on the Congress platform, young Jawaharlal became "a pure nationalist." The Irish Easter Rebellion of 1916 agitated his mind: "For was not that true courage which mocked at almost certain failure and proclaimed to the world that no physical might could crush the invincible spirit of a nation?"

At the end of the war, instead of redeeming their promise of self-government, the British Government committed massacre at Jallianwala Bagh near Amritsar in 1919, by firing 1,600 rounds of ammunition on unarmed peaceful demonstrators. Hundreds of Indians were killed and thousands were wounded. The nation was outraged at this tragedy.[12] Poet Rabindranath Tagore renounced his British Knighthood in protest. Motilal Nehru who was a pro-British Congress Moderate shifted towards the nationalists. Abandoning his profession as a lawyer as being incompatible with public work in a colonial situation, young Jawaharlal, recently married, plunged into national politics, as a full-time Congress worker. The Congress organized relief for the victims and survivors of the Punjab massacre, and also instituted a Committee of Inquiry, to which Jawaharlal was appointed a deputy. During the Committee's work, Jawaharlal saw a great deal of Gandhi: "Very often his (Gandhi's) proposals seemed novel to our Committee and it did not approve of them. But almost always he argued his way to their acceptance and subsequent events showed the wisdom of his advice. Faith in his political insight grew in me."[13] When the Congress met that year at Amritsar, a new slogan "*Mahatma Gandhi ki jai*" (Victory to Mahatma Gandhi) began to dominate the political horizon.

B. *Satyagrahi.* In the next decade Jawaharlal became more and more involved in Gandhian programs. Gandhi had achieved some success with the agrarian movement at Champaran (Behar) and at Kaira (Gujarat). In 1920 Jawaharlal joined the *kisan* (peasant) movement in his province and was shocked to discover the conditions in the villages: "I was filled with shame and sorrow, shame at my own easy-going and comfortable life and our petty politics of the city which ignored this vast multitude of semi-naked sons and daughters of India, sorrow at the degradation and overwhelming poverty of India. A new picture of India seemed to rise before me, naked starving, crushed and utterly miserable. And their faith in us, casual visitors from a distant city, embarrassed me and filled me with a new responsibility that frightened me."[14] This mingling with the peasants and in their affairs gave Jawaharlal something, which English education had failed to do, confidence as a public speaker: "The peasants took away the shyness from me and taught me to speak in public. I spoke to them man to man, and told them what I had in my mind and in heart. Whether the gathering consisted of a few persons or of ten thousand or more, I stuck to my conversational and rather personal method of speaking."[15] This technique Jawaharlal used successfully throughout his political life, both nationally and internationally. His statements and speeches, most often, remained conversational, speaking aloud his thoughts rather than delivering rhetorical exercises.

Rural India made Jawaharlal aware of the mass undercurrent of India's ageless life. At the same time, he became exposed to two other strong influences: one, the cultural aristocracy of Rabindranath Tagore; and second, the social and moral democracy of Gandhi. Tagore's vision of renascent India became translated in the resurrection of ancient Indian tradition of sages and *rishis* and the *gurukula ashrams*, in the life and work at Santiniketan. This educational philosophy challenging the encroaching industrialism and the growing alienation of man from his roots, sought to synthesize man's experience in the simplicity of life and the blessings of natural environment. Gandhi, on the other hand, claiming to be "a practical idealist," emphasized action and spirituality as being the extension of the same experience. His view of life became symbolized in the reform programs, revolutionary methods, and prayer meetings, under the generalized concept of satyagraha (truth force).

Gandhi firmly believed that "nonviolence is the law of our species as violence is the law of the brute,"[16] a position which neither Lao-Tzu, Buddha, nor Jesus, or for that matter any moral guru or prophet of the world would dispute. Yet Gandhi argued that if there were to be "a choice between cowardice and violence, I would advise violence . . . I would rather have India resort to arms in order to defend her honour than that she should in a cowardly manner become or remain a helpless victim to her dishonour. For a mouse hardly forgives a cat when it allows itself to be torn to pieces by her."[17] The reason for Gandhi's implicit faith in his method was that he did not believe India to be helpless. Consequently, Satyagraha and its offshoots, civil disobedience and noncooperation with evil, in spite of their negative connotations, were nothing but new names for the ancient law of suffering.

Gandhi had implicit faith in his perception of truth in his apparently self-contradictory doctrine, a contradiction co-extensive with life itself. But for Jawaharlal these arguments and techniques were challenging means to an end. "We were moved," he wrote, "by these arguments, but for us and for the National Congress as a whole, the non-violent method was not and could not be a religion or an unchallengeable creed or dogma. It could only be a policy and a method promising certain results, and by these results it would have to be finally judged. Individuals might make of it a religion or incontrovertible creed. But no political organization, so long as it remained political, could do so."[18] Thus in spite of his acceptance of Gandhian method, Jawaharlal was not completely a Gandhian but essentially remained a political humanist, unable to disbelieve in the magic enchantment of Gandhi's satyagraha, yet without total commitment to it—an attitude partially based on the definition of faith which he formulated in his school days.

C. *Prisoner*. To be a nationalist in colonial India and demand freedom was a traitorous activity from the British point of view. For this crime unnumbered Indians were beaten, arrested, tried, imprisoned, exiled, tortured, and shot dead. Jawaharlal had his full share of suffering along with others in the process of decolonization.

Jawaharlal was first arrested in Allahabad on December 6, 1920, tried, and imprisoned for six months, for taking part in Gandhi's civil disobedience movement. This process of dehumanization of freedom fighters was repeated in his case eight more times during the next twenty years with increasing severity.

In the first flush of the civil disobedience movement "at least three hundred thousand men and women of India were turned inside the prison gate for political offenses"[19]. In the crowded prisons, life was difficult. Political and social workers of the Congress grew accustomed to the harsh realities of colonial justice and the British Indian prisons. "It was a story of violence," Jawaharlal wrote. Apart from the brutality, corruption, and physical suffering, "the utter want of privacy all day and night became more and more difficult to endure"[20]. During those long periods of imprisonment, Jawaharlal confesses, "reading was my principal occupation."[21] At other times he observed nature very closely through the chinks in the wall and let his mind wander out of prison to distant hills, valleys, and clouds in the sky. In one prison he started digging in the earth and making flower beds. Whenever paper was made available and he had the compulsion, Jawaharlal wrote his thoughts and reactions to events in India and the world, thus contributing to prison literature in English.

D. *Mayor*. In 1923 while Jawaharlal was already the Secretary of U.P. Provincial Congress, he was elected the Mayor of Allahabad, his hometown. He welcomed the opportunity of municipal work, but later on he found out that an Indian mayor was powerless to bring about any changes in the situation or increase services to the Indian community under tight British control. Toward the end of 1923 Jawaharlal was also made the Secretary of the All–India Congress Committee. In spite of his having three jobs, he was without income and this bothered him. But his father insisted that Jawaharlal continue his national work while Motilal earned enough to maintain the family. Because Jawaharlal was tied to the municipal work, he was at home for longer periods than before and found a "great deal of solace and happiness in the family," with his wife, Kamala, and six-year-old daughter, Indira. But this too soon came to an end as more arrests and imprisonments followed.

E. *Frustrated Nationalist*. While most of the congressmen were suffering in the prison, all sorts of persons got into the Congress and changed its policy from opposition to cooperation with the colonial government, and at times directly supported it in its imperial policy. In his agony Jawaharlal heard and read of these betrayals of the Indian cause by Indian agents of the British Empire. In order to break the backbone of the Congress, the British government had fostered the communal antagonism through subtle pressures, support, and patronage, with the result the minorities question became the paramount issue on the national scene and the demand for independence was put in the cold storage.

In these British maneuvers, Jawaharlal clearly saw that the root cause behind communal tensions was not really religion but economic disparity and exploitation. Having directed the politicians to religious rivalries to generate communal riots, the colonial government found itself in the mischievous position of trustees and guardians of individual rights and freedom of the minorities.

The freedom movement in India was not as simple as the freedom movement in the American colonies or in Ireland; they were fighting against the external political power, the imperial British government. Nor was it a straightforward struggle like the struggle of the French or the Russian peoples against their own feudal, aristocratic minority which had reduced them to serfdom; in those countries, the masses had to rise and fight against the government of their own countries, unsupported by an external political and military power, or economic interest.

The Indian nation was struggling to liberate itself from three enemies at the same time. There was obviously the foreign colonial government against which both the American colonists and the Irish nationalists fought in earlier periods with success and achieved their independence. But the foreign colonial government in India was also entrenched in two other power structures in the country. One was the feudal establishment represented by Nawabs, Maharajas, and Zamindars, which was supported and maintained by the British as a necessary bulwark of the Empire. The other power structure was that of the Indian capitalists who, collaborating with international capitalists, allowed the exploitation of India to grow under the feudal set-up within colonial government, and whom the British honored with titles of Knights of the British Empire. Consequently, the people of India had to extricate themselves from these triple tyrannies, each supporting the others in the common oppressive cause.

Whether inside the prison or outside, Jawaharlal found that there was not much he could do toward the achievement of the goal of Indian independence. The imperial policies laid obstacles on every path and they were formidable. Whatever action he took, the colonial law would grab him immediately and cast him in prison. The economic crippling of his family by levying heavy political fines and confiscating household goods and furniture in payment of those fines, the physical hardship of the prison life, and the mental anguish at the frustration of political goals, all made Jawaharlal's life the harder to bear. Added to this, Kamala was growing seriously ill on account of the ill-treatment given to her by the British in the prison. When further medical care for Kamala was recommended, possibly in Switzerland, Jawaharlal welcomed the idea, for he wanted "an excuse to go out of India." He thought perhaps, if he were to go away for some time, from the scene of action, he "could see things in a better perspective and lighten up dark corners" of his mind.[22]

At the beginning of March 1926, Jawaharlal took his sick wife and his little daughter, and sailed from Bombay to Venice, accompanied by Vijayalakshmi and her husband, Ranjit Pundit.

IV *Congress Envoy, 1926–27*

Jawaharlal went to Europe only for a couple of months to take care of his ailing wife, but his stay was prolonged for twenty-one months. During that period, he was educated in Europe in the practical art of international politics, mainly arising out of the conflicts of colonialism and capitalism and their offshoots, socialism and communism. This exposure provided Jawaharlal with a vantage point, to view the Indian struggle for freedom in the context of European conflicts; in this situation he was placed as the envoy extraordinary of voiceless India on international platforms.

In 1926 Jawaharlal was returning to a different Europe from the one he had seen in his school days in 1905–12. Since then the continent had witnessed intense colonial rivalries resulting in World War 1 in 1914–18, and the subsequent scramble for the spoils of war by the imperial powers, chiefly Britain and France. A socio-economic philosophy which evolved in Western Europe had been put to practice through a revolution in Eastern Europe. The continent was going through the birth pangs of a new way of life and economic reconstruction based on social justice. The application of this philosophy was achieved with comparative ease in Scandinavian countries having neither the tradition of slavery nor serfs nor colonies; with forced labor and autocratic policy in the conglomerate nationalities of the Soviet Union; with bitter labor unrest against tyrannical capital in other parts of Europe.

Yet the imperial British propaganda characterized this philosophy of social justice as dangerous to the empire and therefore seditious in the colonies. What was threatened by that philosophy was not the poverty of the masses but the profits of the colonists and the disproportionate accumulation of economic gains by the feudal lords, under the protection of the empire.

In his experience with the European dilemma of being democratic at home and imperialistic abroad, Jawaharlal saw that the demand for independence was not a particular urge of the Indian masses but a world-wide movement of oppressed peoples who were deprived of their inherent right to be free in their own homeland and shape their own well-being. This identification of Indian national movement with international struggle provided him with a clearer perspective to view the problems and difficulties involved in the process of decolonization. Since the political and economic issues were tied to the military apparatus of the dominating powers like Britain, France, Belgium, Netherlands, and U.S., these powers primarily abetted and aided, sympathized and supported each other to preserve the status quo. Consequently India was not fighting an isolated, over-extended political institution from a little island in the North Atlantic but a whole brotherhood of colonizers and imperial adversaries.

Jawaharlal's primary concentration revolved round the question of how to extricate India from the innumerable colonial bonds which Britain had tied during the last two centuries, from the days of suppliant traders to the time of arrogant imperial power. These shackles were added, one by one, not only for the subjugation of the nation but also for the exploitation of its resources for the benefit of the imperial country, and most subtly, the bonds for the cultural subordination of the ruling upper class Indians to the necessities of the empire, namely enforcing "law and order" among Kipling's "lawless tribes." Whether those bonds could be severed without a violent break, whether the so-called democratic Britain which conquered with ruthless violence would willingly give up its political and military power, and the source of its enormous wealth, simply because some English-educated Moderates and Liberals annually met and passed pious resolutions, or, in fact, whether any nation would ever obtain freedom by the mere fact of asking for it, which never happened in Europe or America—these and many other questions began to agitate Jawaharlal's mind. In the light of this it seemed inevitable that it was necessary to realize one's own identity lying submerged and dormant under the glittering canopy of the empire before the national aspirations could fructify into any meaningful struggle.

The early months of his stay in Europe, Jawaharlal spent in Geneva where he became interested in the activities of the League of Nations and the International Labor Office. These two organizations had some of the aroma of utopian promise to nations under colonial rule and workers suffering under severe economic disadvantage. He visited England during the General Strike of 1926 and was shocked to see the conditions of coal miners in Derbyshire and the farce of the judicial process under which they were harrassed, and apparently tortured. While in Geneva Jawaharlal also came in contact with many distinguished European and American liberal thinkers, scientists and men of high purpose, dedicated to the service of man, hoping to relieve man's lot from man-made miseries. Among them were Ernest Toller, the young German poet and dramatist and an earnest socialist; Roger Baldwin of the Civil Liberties Union in New York: Frank Buckmann of the Oxford Group movement (later on called Moral Re-Armament, with a typically imperial mentality); Romain Rolland, the French philosopher; Albert Einstein, the great scientist-humanitarian; and many Indian exiles.

Towards the end of 1926 Jawaharlal was in Berlin which was then the European headquarters for all radicals from abroad. Having lost her colonies after the war, Germany was viewing with benevolent neutrality the growth of agitation in the colonies of other powers and, in fact, was giving shelter from the British Secret Service to many exiles from Asia and Africa. These nationalist exiles thought of some joint actions between the oppressed nations *inter se* and the labor organizations against the colonial-capitalist powers. Consequently a Congress of Oppressed Nationalities was convened to be held in Brussels in early February 1927. When the Indian National Congress came to know about it, Jawaharlal was appointed as the official delegate.

The Congress met in Brussels on February 10, under the presidency of George Lansbury of the British Labour Party, attended by representatives of countries of Asia, Africa, and Latin America. Jawaharlal met many of these nationalists leaders and labor leaders and was reinforced in his conviction that the freedom movement was an international movement. The Brussels Congress brought about a basic realization that colonialism and capitalism were basically creating the same problems in different countries, namely suppressing the freedom of the people by reinforcing decaying elements of feudal, tribal, or autocratic rule and thus preventing the natural evolution of socio-political and economic institutions suited to the needs of the people; that the forces of change in the colonies were branded as "subversive", "seditious", "conspiratorial", "leftist", or "communist" in a somewhat derogatory sense, with a view to create a sense of fear, resulting in a kind of witch hunt. Thus the progressive ideologies of social justice developed in Western Europe were equated and denounced as being the same thing as Russian imperialism!

As far as the oppressed people were concerned there was not much to choose between West or East European aggressive intentions, exploitation by colonial capitalism or communism, between the missionary and proselytizing zeal of capitalist or communist subversion. What was urgently needed was the containment of international capitalism and colonialism to prevent international communism following in their wake, and this could only be done by upholding national and economic independence of the oppressed people. The Brussels Congress established a sense of common bond and solidarity among people of different races, cultures, and continents suffering at the hands of a common enemy. This sense of solidarity was an important achievement, a kind of a moral boost which reexpressed itself in the Bandung Conference of nonaligned nations three decades later in the 1950's and in the spirit of Geneva-77 in the 1960's

Before the termination of the conference, a permanent executive body was formed under the name, The League Against Imperialism, which Lansbury agreed to chair. Jawaharlal was elected a member of this organization along with Madame Sun Yat-Sen, Romain Rolland, and Albert Einstein. It was for the first time that Jawaharlal was recognized internationally as a spokesman for a large section of the oppressed people.

In the summer of 1927 when Jawaharlal and Motilal were in Berlin, they received invitations from the Soviet government to visit Moscow and participate in the Tenth Jubilee celebrations of the Soviet Revolution. In response the Nehru family—Motilal, Jawaharlal, Kamala, Indira, and Krishna (Jawaharlal's younger sister)— traveled by train via Warsaw and visited Moscow for four days during November 7–10, 1927. In early December Jawaharlal returned with his family to India in time to attend the Indian National Congress held in Madras.

V *National Leader, 1927–1935*

A. *Congress Executive.* After his European experience, with wider outlook on national and international politics, and a clearer perception of the socio-economic elements of the conflicts, Jawaharlal could not disassociate himself or the Indian national movement from the international struggle. He realized that his immediate task in India was, first to disagree with the moderates, including his father, and discard the political goal of dominion status within the British

Empire; secondly, to make the Indian National Congress demand full and complete independence for India, even at the risk of disagreeing with Gandhi, however drastic and extreme that demand might be; and thirdly, to train and prepare congressmen, labor leaders, youth, in fact, the whole country "for these world events."

In pursuit of these goals Jawaharlal began to assert his own point of view in Indian national affairs and international fronts, thus displaying his independence and maturity in the Congress. At the Congress session held in December 1927 at Madras, Jawaharlal moved a resolution making complete independence the Congress goal.[23] The resolution was passed in spite of the opposition of the moderates while Gandhi thought he was "going too fast," and the resolution was too premature and was something of a "school-boy type resolution." The Congress approved this "academic resolution" in order to get rid of it and then "to move on to something more important."[24]

In spite of his affront to the Congress executive, Jawaharlal was elected the Secretary of the Congress in 1928, and the President in 1929. By occupying these high offices, he brought about a shift in the Congress policy from willingness to cooperate with the colonial government to accept dominion status to that of demanding complete independence. The British government could not tolerate such a revolutionary leader. Consequently, he was imprisoned continually. But the more the British government imprisoned and suppressed Jawaharlal, the more he grew in stature and expressed his thoughts. Whenever he was out of prison, he issued statements, made speeches, and directed Congress work; but when he was deprived of these channels for action, Jawaharlal expressed his thoughts and visions, and also his sufferings and hopes of triumphs in an amazing body of prison literature, emerging from the cell of his imprisoned soul, reaching out to the larger humanity outside.

B. *The Writer*. At the Brussels Congress, Jawaharlal realized that India should actively seek the support of and cooperate with freedom movements in other countries. But such international contacts were either stifled or deliberately restricted by the British government. To persuade the Congress and urge the nation, he wrote an article, "India and the Need for International Contacts," setting out various means available to them, and the advantages of such contacts.[25]

In response to numerous inquires about the causes and consequences of the Soviet Revolution and how it could help India to overthrow colonial government, reorganize feudal institutions, and liquidate capitalistic monopoly, Jawaharlal wrote a series of articles giving his impressions of his visit to Moscow in November 1927, and his considered opinions derived from his acquaintance with both anti- and pro-Soviet books and points of view. These "Random Sketches and Impressions" were published under the title, *Soviet Russia* (Allahabad, 1928).

In the summer of 1928 when Jawaharlal was occupied with the work of the Congress as its General Secretary at Allahabad, his little daughter, Indira, was at a hill-station in Mussoorie in the Himalayas. As a diversion, Jawaharlal wrote a series of letters telling her the prehistoric story of the world; these letters published under the name, *Letters from a Father to His Daughter* (Allahabad, 1930), became a charming contribution to children's literature. During his imprisonments for the fifth and sixth times between 1930–33, he wrote another series of 196 letters to his daughter, telling her the story of the world and many people who occupied it during the historic period. They were put together in two volumes under the heading *Glimpses of World History* (Allahabad, 1934).

As soon as Jawaharlal was out of prison he wrote a position paper, surveying the political situation, *Whither India?* (Allahabad, 1934). Thereafter he continued to issue statements of policy, or press releases, or answers to criticisms. Some of the significant pieces of writing were collected under the title, *Recent Essays and Writings* (Allahabad, 1934).

Before long Jawaharlal was imprisoned for the seventh time, another long two-year term, 1934–35. At that time he was undergoing a personal and family crisis. In his anguish he wrote a testament of his faith in his celebrated *An Autobiography* (London, 1936). Some British friends of India desiring to educate the British public and the British colonial government and enlighten them on the aspirations of the Indian people, commissioned H. G. Alexander to edit a volume containing Jawaharlal's important statements and writings. This volume was published under the name, *India and the World* (London, 1936).

While Jawaharlal was still undergoing his seventh term in prison, Kamala was taken seriously ill in May 1935, and was taken to Germany for treatment by family friends. When Jawaharlal was finally released on September 4, 1935, he rushed to Europe to be with his wife. He moved her from Badenweiler, Germany to Lausanne, Switzerland but her condition progressively deteriorated. Kamala lingered for a few more weeks and died on February 28, 1936, and Jawaharlal returned to India with an urn containing her ashes.

IV   *International Spokesman, 1936–46*

After many frustrating attempts to negotiate with the British government for the so-called dominion status, and the failures of three round-table conferences held in London, the Congress finally came to the conclusion that there was no alternative to Jawaharlal's unqualified demand for complete independence. Gandhi had great faith in human nature, and insisted that the British were a civilized nation and they could be persuaded to accept India's demand to be free. Yet that freedom was nowhere near. While Jawaharlal was still in Europe attending to Kamala's illness, the National Congress, as if to rectify its own errors in policy, elected Jawaharlal to be the President once again in 1936, and re-elected him in 1937.

During those hectic years while occupying the highest position in the Congress, Jawaharlal carried the demand for freedom to lands beyond India's borders. He was pained to see the suppression of freedom by fascist powers, with the support of the imperial powers, in Czechoslovakia, Ethiopia, Spain, and China. He visited those countries, and spoke and acted in support of the people and their freedom struggles. He also visited the neighboring countries of Ceylon, Burma and Malaya assuring them of the solidarity in the common struggle and at the same time developing international relations. His writings and statements of this period were published in two volumes: *Eighteen Months in India* (Allahabad, 1938), and *China, Spain, and the War* (Allahabad, 1940).

In 1939, Britain declared war and dragged India along with her into belligerency. Consequently, all the Indian national leaders were arrested and put in prison. Jawaharlal was imprisoned for the eighth time for over a year. While he was in prison, the voice of the Congress was made audible in London by the indefatigable V. K. Krishna Menon with his vocal India League and its powerful membership. To reinforce his campaign in the British capital, Krishna Menon edited a volume of Jawaharlal's collected writings, speeches and statements from 1937–41, under the heading, *The Unity of India* (London, 1941).

When the British empire in Asia was beginning to collapse at the Japanese advance, Britain released Indian leaders, expecting them to cooperate in the British war efforts without any promise of independence after the war. Gandhi demanded the formation of a national government in India but Britain wanted the absolute control of the colony and its economy. When the retreating British army initiated a scorched earth policy in Eastern India and started burning Indian national resources, produce and people, Gandhi in his anguish discarding all efforts at negotiations, moved the famous "Quit India" Resolution at the Congress session in Bombay on August 8, 1942. The British government responded with massive arrests of all leaders of the Congress and its subsidiary organizations. Jawaharlal was imprisoned without trial for the ninth time and the longest period of three years, 1942–45. It was during this confinement that Jawaharlal entered an intense period of examining national identity, and wrote over a thousand pages in five months. This labor of love, stopped for lack of paper, was later put together with the help of his daughter, Indira, and was published after Jawaharlal's release, under the title, *The Discovery of India* (Calcutta, 1946).

VII   *Prime Minister, 1946–1964*

As the war came to an end, the Indian leaders were released once again and were called to a conference at Simla in 1945; arrangements were made for the transfer of power, not without hammering a wedge in the unity of the nation. Britain decided to partition India under an outdated medieval theocratic two-nation theory, resulting in unprecedented communal riots, and mass-migration of refugees. In the transfer of power Jawaharlal was elected to be the chief executive or the Prime Minister of the provisional government of India (1945–47); and thereafter of independent India (1947–50). When a constitution was adopted and India was declared a republic, Jawaharlal was once again elected to be the Prime Minister of the Republic of India, which office he held until his death on May 27, 1964.

In 1946, after he became the chief executive of the Indian government, Jawaharlal was more involved in making history than writing about it. He neither had the leisure nor the luxury of isolation, for reflective thought and unhurried time to write, as he had when he was in prison. His imprisonments, though they were meant to suppress him, had produced the opposite effect. By translating his thoughts and visions, the nature of his intense personal conflicts and the collective national struggle of the people into written books, he not only transcended prison walls and reached the hearts of millions of people in India and abroad, but also left behind a legacy of prison literature, unique in the circumstance of its production, extraordinary in its point of view, and vibrating with the spirit of a man of renaissance sensibilities. By writing a dozen books in English Jawaharlal also secured a place for himself in the community of world authors.

CHAPTER 2

Early Writings: Statements, Speeches, and Writings (*1929*)

A S soon as Jawaharlal Nehru was elected President of the Indian National Congress in 1928, there was much curiosity and public interest about the thinking of the chief executive of the national freedom movement. Anticipating this demand, L. Ram Mohan Lal compiled Jawaharlal's early writings and speeches, covering the period from 1922 to 1928 when he was only a congressman and less known on the political scene of the country. The book was published by the University and National Book supplies, Allahabad, in 1929 under the title, *Pandit Jawaharlal Nehru: Statements, Speeches, and Writings*, with an appreciation by Mahatma Gandhi.

In the preface, the publishers state that their purpose in issuing the volume was two fold: first, Jawaharlal, being "the first socialist to preside over the Indian National Congress," had a message to give to his country, and that message had to be made clear to the public; second, Jawaharlal's thinking represented a new trend in the Indian freedom movement, which was "in many respects different and in some respects opposed to that of his predecessors." In the light of this dramatic shift in the Congress position, the publisher felt Jawaharlal's statements and writings containing seeds of his thoughts became very significant especially "at the critical juncture in the country's affairs."[1]

The first collected works of young Jawaharlal included two written statements made by him at his own trial in 1922 and 1923; an article, "India and the Need for International Contacts," published in *New Era*; the epoch-making independence resolution and his statement thereon, delivered to the Congress session in 1927 at Madras; six presidential addresses, and three other speeches.

I *Colonial Justice*

Jawaharlal's two written defences at his own trials are less in the nature of legalistic documents and more in the nature of idealistic statements of a daring young revolutionary. Having acquired "most of the prejudices of Harrow and Cambridge," he stated, he could not participate in the so-called political trials amounting to some kind of a farce. Instead, Jawaharlal indicted the system of judicature established under a colonial government, since no such system functioning under imperial decrees and ordinances could deliver "justice" to the freedom fighters among the colonial people.

The first statement, dated May 17, 1922, was read in the court in Allahabad when Jawaharlal was tried for participating in Gandhi's Swadeshi (Home Made Products) Movement and the boycott of British goods. Jawaharlal argued that "the evils and the misery and the poverty" caused by the dumping of British goods in a "long-suffering country" are manifold, and such unequal trade practices imposed under colonial rule have to be rectified for the "salvation of India and her hungry millions" (pp. 7–8). Consequently, he maintained that sedition against the British government "has become the creed of the Indian people; to preach and practice disaffection against the evil which it represents, has become their chief occupation" (p. 3).

Even though Jawaharlal pointed out that under the law "in India as in England, peaceful picketing is no crime," the colonial judge found sufficient justification to sentence him to eighteen months' rigorous imprisonment. The British judge was more concerned with granting protection to the imperial monopoly trade than relieving the misery it created in the colony by draining it economically. As Jawaharlal argued, the British industry got "justice" more than the Indian people did.

Somewhat anticipating the decision of the court, Jawaharlal had pointed out in his statement that, on account of the nature of the struggle involved to free the nation from imperial bonds, "jail had indeed become a holy place of pilgrimage," and many people volunteered for such a sacrifice. Speaking for himself and other Indian patriots victimized under the judicial machinery of a colonizing power, Jawaharlal stated: "We suffer ourselves and by our suffering seek to convert our adversary" (p. 4). The dream of "brave deeds, with sword in hand" of his school days had been transformed into a brave collective suffering to redeem the oppressor. This warrior without a sword had optimistically voiced the *mantra* of the age when he declared: "I shall go with the conviction that I shall come out to greet *Swaraj* (self-rule) in India" (p. 11). But it took another twenty long years of suffering for that conviction to become a reality, for the British government to finally get the meaning of such self-sacrificing resolve of Gandhian Satyagrahis.

The second statement to the court, dated October 3, 1923, was issued by Jawaharlal at a fictitious trial in Nabha State, framed by the British political agent when Jawaharlal entered that state. The political agent, as was customary in those days, having usurped the powers of the state by deposing the maharaja, was acting like a tin-pot dictator, "under the sheltering wings of the British Government" (p. 22). The trial, in fact, had no reference to any law. Jawaharlal made his written statement to expose "the very unscrupulousness and immorality of the proceedings," apparently initiated to keep Jawaharlal behind the bars under some pseudo-judicial pretext. After exposing the false nature of the charge, Jawaharlal observed, "justice, or even a strict observance of the law has little to do with political trials in India" (p. 12).

II   *International Contacts*

During his twenty-one month European trip in 1926–27, Jawaharlal observed the conditions in India under the British colonial rule from many perspectives. First, from the headquarters of the League of Nations in Geneva, which was established to support the aspirations of non-self-governing people throughout the world for self-determination; second, from the liberal and socialistic points of view from Paris, Berlin, London, and Moscow; third, from the point of view of the Brussels Congress of Opressed Nationalities, attended by labor and trade union leaders from all over the world, and nationalist leaders from colonized countries of Asia, Africa and Latin America; and finally, from the point of view of Indian nationalists in exile taking shelter in Germany and Switzerland to escape the ever pursuing British Secret Service.[2] These experiences not only gave him a new and valuable insight into some of the problems created by the brotherhood of international capitalism and colonialism, but also the realization that such an amalgam is the common foe of all the oppressed peoples in the world.

On his return to India, Jawaharlal, more than any other leader, identified the Indian freedom struggle as part of the larger world-wide struggle of undoing European and Anglo-American domination outside Europe and North America. It was in this context that he conceived his role in the work of the Congress and felt that India must have international contacts with people suffering under predicaments similar to those of herself. For such contacts, he felt, would strengthen and consolidate the surging movement of the oppressed peoples. To this end he wrote an article, "India and the Need for International Contacts," which was published in the *New Era* in 1928.

In his article, Jawaharlal maintained that the struggle for "the freedom of India becomes an essential condition for world freedom" (p. 115). Since the freedom movements are not the cause of world unrest but only the consequences of the previous suppression of freedom by the dominating powers, Jawaharlal felt that the world peace could only be maintained by a process of decolonization, and by trimming the dominating tendencies of aggressive nations. For such purpose there needs to be an international "super-state to which all nations will owe allegiance, or . . . a cooperative world commonwealth" (p. 114). In such idealistic dreams, Jawaharlal saw his political vision, almost twenty years before the establishment of the United Nations, and even after India's independence, he translated it in terms of his unique nonalignment policy.

While the political ideal remained a distant goal, Jawaharlal saw the immediate necessity for oppressed peoples to join together and consolidate their struggle; for he pointed out such contacts were not developed, or prevented from developing by the colonizing powers. In India, the British had so conditioned the country to recognize the outside world through British colonial spectacles that the nation was duped to identify the enemies of British empire as the enemies of India! "We have seen the world," wrote Jawaharlal, "through English eyes and with English prejudices" (p. 119).

To rectify this imbalance in India's external relations, and to "get out of the curious mentality of subservience to England," Jawaharlal advocated that the Congress should develop international contacts of its own (even at the risk of incurring the displeasure of the British government), with countries other than Britain and British colonies, so as to view the world and absorb current world developments from an Indian perspective. Such initiatives, he urged, were advocated by India's friends at home and abroad to enable India to "appreciate the forces that are moulding the world today." He pointed out that "some of them tell us that we should cooperate with all other anti-imperial forces to combat imperialism; others favour an Asiatic federation; while a third group are sanguine enough to want us to utilize the machinery of the League of Nations for our benefit" (p. 115).

Jawaharlal had no illusions about such international contacts; he realized that there "is little of charity in international dealings, and no country can make good except through its own efforts." Yet he strongly felt that such contacts would be beneficial to India struggling to be free, and to future independent India which will have to find its own destiny among the comity of nations, with its own independent foreign policy.

Jawaharlal who had spent seven years in England for his education and twenty-one months in Europe acquiring experience in international politics, found the main cause for India's mental subordination to Britain was Macaulay's notorious policy of "English Education," imposed on the nation since 1835. The restrictive curriculum in Indian universities and schools, rigidly controlled by the British government, the choice of subjects taught, the method of "teaching foreign languages through the stepmother tongue" English instead of the mother tongues, all these made it virtually impossible to divert the stream of Indian students, teachers, professors, educators and others from England to other countries for higher studies. Jawaharlal felt that "the offensive social atmosphere which an Indian has to encounter in England" as a colonial, and "mere self-respect ought to have been sufficient to induce our students to keep away from England" (p. 125).

Although Jawaharlal perceived, almost twenty years before independence, that India's mental enslavement was worse than political subordination, he did not do anything meaningful to remove the root cause or to change the situation. Even twenty years after independence, Indian universities continue to enforce the restricted curriculum, teach foreign languages through the "stepmother tongue," and look at the world through English spectacles. Obviously, a revolution by consent, such as the transfer of power in India, has the drawback of not changing the fundamental thinking, but only superficially replacing the political apparatus and super-structure, while the colonial attitudes indoctrinated, and the machinery for such indoctrination, continue to operate smoothly by the efforts of Indians themselves.

III   *Complete Independence*

In the early 1920's the Indian freedom movement was somewhat thwarted in its initial stage on account of the split in the Congress among the Moderates and the Liberals supporting the British status quo with slight marginal reforms, those seeking some kind of self-rule backed by Gandhian movement of non-cooperation with the foreign government, and the extreme position spearheaded by Jawaharlal demanding complete independence. While the Moderates and the Liberals voiced the British opinion that the difference of opinion in the Congress was healthy, Jawaharlal felt strongly that there could be no two opinions on the question of Indian independence, and he wanted the Congress to demand it in a single unanimous voice. He expressed his frustration at what he considered as the diabolical action of the colonial government in fostering a deliberate split in the national movement in the name of importing west European "political methods and manoeuvers," and thus hoisting the so-called Indian opposition to the Indian demand for complete independence! (p. 27).

Jawaharlal scoffed at the British offer of "provincial autonomy" in place of freedom. The Moderates and the Liberals being subservient to the British were willing to accept such vague promises, for they did not dare openly to demand complete freedom from their rulers. In his impatience Jawaharlal expressed his hope as early as 1923 that "I shall welcome the day when the Congress declares for independence" (p. 29). But then he was a lonely voice and a nonentity. Yet such a resolve was almost forced upon the Congress five years later when Jawaharlal, after his return from Europe, in a dramatic move suddenly proposed his famous resolution for complete independence at the Madras session in December 1927. The resolution simply reads in clear and unmistakable English: "The Congress declares the goal of the Indian people to be complete independence" (p. 93). This simple and straightforward resolution was only excelled by yet another crisper statement by Gandhi fifteen years later in 1942, demanding that the British "Quit India!"

In moving his Complete Independence Resolution, Jawaharlal was challenging the authority of the elder statesmen in the Congress, including his father Motilal; he was also opposing Gandhi and his supporters in the slow-moving Non-cooperation Movement who were thinking of a "dominion status," or some kind of home rule of the type which the British government evasively promised to Ireland but did not actually grant. To all of them Jawaharlal made his intentions clear that the resolution "means what it says. It means complete independence. It means control of the defence forces of the country. It means control over the financial and economic policy of the country. It means control over the relations with the foreign countries. Without these things, independence would be a travesty and a camouflage" (p. 94).

Yet the fact that there were in 1928 English-educated Indians to oppose the demand for complete independence for India, Jawaharlal argued, amply demonstrated how "the subtle poison of British rule has enervated and emasculated" a significant section of the Indian population (p. 31). In other words, the colonial government continued to oppress the people of India partly because Indians themselves cooperated and helped to sustain it. Jawaharlal felt that the "evil flourishes only because we tolerate it and assist in it; the most despotic and tyrannical government can only carry on because the people it misgoverns themselves submit to it" (p. 30).

Optimistically Jawaharlal hoped that his resolution should be "the immediate goal and not a goal for the far distant future," as some Moderates had tried to suggest (p. 94). He put the burden of achieving that goal on the Congress itself; "Whether we achieve it today or tomorrow, or a year hence or ten years hence, I cannot say. That depends on your strength and the strength of the country" (p. 94). Yet he was conscious of this goal of complete independence many years before he moved the resolution at the Congress session. His resolve was crystallized in the voluntary suffering during the Swadeshi movement when he was arrested, tried, and imprisoned in Allahabad in 1922. At that time, before going to prison, he had declared in the Court: "I shall go with the conviction that I shall come out to greet *Swaraj* [freedom] in India" (p. 11). Such a resolve was strengthened as he spoke at Benares in 1923 when he prophetically declared, "I am convinced that political freedom will come to us before long, if not entirely through our strength, then through the weakness of Europe and England" (p. 38).

IV *Social and Economic Reorganization*

During this decade Jawaharlal showed considerable awareness of some of the basic problems which a liberated nation would face. He posed the question before the Congress in 1928: "What manner of independence is it which results in starvation for many and the exploitation of the millions?" (p. 42). Since the full content of the concept of freedom involved elimination of all exploitation, Jawaharlal warned, "you must attack everything in your society which helps the foreign and domestic exploiter." Such actions could not be taken either under the provincial autonomy or dominion status which the British were actively canvassing in order to keep India within the empire. That was a powerful reason, Jawaharlal argued, why India should demand nothing less than complete independence so that the nation could take vigorous action to overcome the existing inequities in social and economic matters.

Jawaharlal recognized the hidden dangers involved in the domestic feudalism and foreign colonialism collaborating with international and Indian capitalistic class. Since "the masses really are the nation" and on "their prosperity depends the prosperity of the country," it was necessary to avoid the pitfall of some of the so-called "leaders" hypocritically betraying the trust of the masses after independence, and stepping into the shoes of the foreign exploiter. In drawing up the program of social and economic reconstruction of the nation, he saw the need to "keep the interests of the masses uppermost, and sacrifice everything else to them." (p. 43).

After independence, however, this noble ideal waned and Jawaharlal was unable to "sacrifice" the vested interests of some of the "leaders" for rehabilitating the jobless and the landless, and they in turn had to resort to extreme measures like the Naxalite movement in the 1970's in order to secure their own freedom from politically independent India.

V *Labor Welfare*

Jawaharlal displayed a good deal of understanding of the lot of Indian workers. During his European trip he had spent a few months in Geneva, familiarizing himself with the work of the International Labor Office. He had talked with leaders of labor and trade unions in Europe and North America, and learned about the progress workers had made in those countries. During the Brussels Congress of the Oppressed Nationalities, he also met leaders of workers from Asia, Africa, and Latin America. When he was in Moscow, he had also seen the benefits the workers enjoyed in Russia. Upon his return to India, Jawaharlal was viewing the lot of Indian workers under British rule against the background of workers' conditions in other countries.

In a presidential address to the All–India Trade Union Congress, held in Nagpur in December 1929, Jawaharlal pointed out that "the spread of industrialism cannot be checked" (p. 61), that what is perhaps not sufficiently realized is "the international character of industrialism" (p. 59). This has led, he argued, to collective colonialism by industrialized countries. Consequently, British imperialism linked to colonial exploitation is not a phenomenon peculiar to the British race, but is a "necessary consequence of industrial development on capitalistic lines" (p. 62).

What Jawaharlal was concerned with was whether India must also "succumb to all the evils which come in the process of capitalistic industrialization," or "is it possible for us to adopt industrialism without its major evils" on the basis of another social order. Jawaharlal felt that the only alternative that offered to India "is some form of socialism," perhaps the Scandinavian type where social justice is achieved by legislative action, and the state regulates the means of production and distribution.[3]

Jawaharlal saw the inadequacy of mere political independence if it did not improve the lot of the worker. "What shall it profit," he asked, "the masses of this country, the peasantry, the landless labourers, the workers, the shopkeepers, the artisans, if every one of the offices held by Englishmen in India today is held by an Indian?" (p. 66). It would only substitute the agents of exploitation. He was convinced that "fundamentally, the condition of the worker cannot be improved until the social fabric is changed" and the only effective change that could be brought about was by the establishment of a democratic socialist state.

VI   *Youth as Social Reformer*

Jawaharlal's idealistic view of the role of youth in society and his own daring sense of adventure in life and politics, made him wear a romantic halo as the symbol of the nation's youth. Besides, he identified the awakening of India's younger generation with the worldwide youth movement.

In his address to student and youth conferences, Jawaharlal argued that the problems of the world were created by older men who "sat in their comfortable cabinets and banking houses and hid their selfishness and greed and lies under a cover of fine phrases and appeals for freedom and democracy" (p. 97). But it is the youth, millions of them, who paid in blood, sweat, and tears in fighting their wars;

it is the youth who got killed and mutilated, "young men with their lives stretching out in front of them and their hopes unfulfilled" (p. 80). Therefore, the youth have the particular obligation to become dissatisfied, and growing restless, rebel against the existing establishment. It is only they who could precipitate changes in the society, since the "youth can think and is not afraid of the consequences of thought" which is in itself "the most revolutionary thing on earth" (p. 82).

From a historical point of view, Jawaharlal maintained that changes in a society were brought about by those who disassociated themselves from the status quo. "It is not the sleek and shiny people having more than their share of this world's goods who are the apostles of change. The world changes and progresses because of those who are disaffected and dissatisfied and who are not prepared to tolerate the evils and injustices of things as they are or have been" (p. 113). Great men of the past who reformed the human societies have always been rebels against the existing orders—Buddha, Confucius, Zarathustra, Moses, Jesus, Mohammed or Nanak. Even so, what is greater than any man is the idea which he has embodied; for the ideas growing like seeds blossom into large societies and civilizations. Consequently, Jawaharlal held "the avatars of today are great ideas which come to reform the world" (p. 92); and the new idea of our time which is fast growing into a formidable avatar is socialism, or the concept of social justice.

Since older men conditioned by older ideas cannot see the ways of new manifestation, he urged that it is for the youth to assimilate the new ideas and become their "instrument to transform the world" from the inequities of older ideas, such as feudalism, capitalism, colonialism, and imperialism, and make the world "a better place to live in" (p. 92). Thus Jawaharlal saw in the youth a higher duty to view the society afresh with new vision, and help it to move from the rut to a healthier state.

Jawaharlal warned that a small group of people "having reserved very magnanimously the Kingdom of Heaven for the poor" have taken good care to "keep the kingdom of earth for themselves" (p. 84). What the poor wanted is to cease to be poor. That can only come by "changing a system which produces poverty and misery." India cannot hope to bring about this much needed social change without changing the mental attitude. "Our elders fail frequently," Jawaharlal complained, "because they are rigid in their minds and unable to change their mental outlook or adapt themselves to changing facts. But youth is not hidebound" (p. 82). He urged the youth to harness their energies to overthrow the colonial rule supported by feudalist and capitalist elements within the society, and to rebuild a new social order in the land which would benefit the millions and the masses.

Though Jawaharlal himself was growing into his middle age and was in the process of joining the elders, he retained not only his youthful dash and enthusiasm, but also his ability to give expression to the thoughts and feelings of the younger generation. In one of his addresses to the youth organizations, Jawaharlal admitted that participation in youth conferences gave him the opportunity to recoup for himself and share in the "abounding hope and courage of the youth" and to take back with him to his daily work "some measure of their faith and their enthusiasm" (p. 132).

Because of Jawaharlal's capacity to communicate with the nation's youth and identify with their aspirations, Mahatma Gandhi, desiring to draw them into the freedom movement, nominated their hero to be "the first socialist president" of the Indian National Congress in 1928. But the Congress executive consisting of grey-haired Moderates and Liberals doubted the choice, for they considered Jawaharlal to be rather rash and naive at the beginning of his political career. Gandhi having declined the presidency for himself, and instead having nominated young Jawaharlal to that high office, was obliged to defend his choice publicly: "In bravery he [Jawaharlal] is not to be surpassed. Who can excel him in the love of the country? 'He is rash and impetuous' say some. This quality is an additional qualification at the present moment. And if he has the dash and the rashness of a warrior, he has also the prudence of a statesman. . . The nation is safe in his hands." (p. ii).

After such an endorsement of the swordless warrior by the prophet of peace, there was no retreating for Jawaharlal from his declared goal of complete independence. It was in this context that the publisher felt the crucial importance of Jawaharlal's thinking, however extreme that may have been, and a need for a collected volume of his speeches and writings, to help the nation see the goal which Jawaharlal had been championing for almost a decade.

CHAPTER 3

Reportage: Soviet Russia (*1928*)

I *Journalist's Report*

JAWAHARLAL'S first book, *Soviet Russia*, was not really written as a book, but as the subtitle suggests, as a series of articles giving "Some Random Sketches and Impressions" of Soviet Russia ten years after the revolution. When the Nehru family was in western Europe in 1926–27, they were invited to visit Moscow for the Tenth Jubilee anniversary celebration of the Soviet Revolution in November 1927. The visit gave Jawaharlal an opportunity to see at first hand some aspects of the workings of "one of the mightiest experiments in history."[1]

After his return to India, Jawaharlal was confronted by his countrymen's continuous hunger for information about the revolutionized Russian society. They were curious to know what caused the sudden dynamism of the Russian people which enabled them to overthrow an imperial government, eliminate the feudal structure of the society, redistribute the land, and extend to the masses social and economic benefits such as compulsory education, medical care and guaranteed employment. They were also interested to know how the Soviet Union withstood outside attempts headed by imperial Britain, at boycott, economic blockade, and a war of intervention to destroy the revolutionized society and its government.

The Indian nationalists in their fight for freedom against imperial Britain were fascinated by the Soviet Revolution and looked up to it in the same manner as the American colonies looked up to the French Revolution for moral support in their struggle for freedom against the same enemy. However, in the twentieth century, Indians could not get much solace either from France or the United States of America, for both nations, having outgrown their revolutionary origins, had become, in fact, imperial powers in their own rights, and had ceased to breathe the aspirations of the French and American revolutionaries; nor could they understand the revolutionary temper of people in other parts of the world.

In response to these demands for information about Soviet Russia, Jawaharlal wrote a series of articles at the risk of possible imprisonment by the British government on the ground that such writings were seditious. The powerful British-owned English newspapers in India, such as *The Times of India* or *The Statesmen*, were already airing the British imperial anti-Soviet propaganda on a hysterical level, almost advocating the overthrow of the Soviet government and the restoration, if possible, of the old imperial Tsardom. Consequently, most of Jawaharlal's articles were published in Indian-owned (and respectable from the British point of view) English papers, such as *The Hindu* of Madras, and Gandhi's *Young India*.

When it was suggested to Jawaharlal that his articles be published in a book form, he was hesitant, For he felt that they were too "disjointed and sketchy," being based on "a little personal knowledge and more on reading," and were mainly written "in railway trains, and . . . sandwiched into the intervals between other activities" as the General Secretary of the Congress. Later he agreed to do so in the hope that the book might answer some of the questions. "I am fully aware," he wrote in a foreword dated October 10, 1928, "that it requires a person of considerable knowledge and some courage to write about the complex and ever-changing conditions of Soviet Russia. I claim no such knowledge and though I may possess the habit of rushing in where wiser people fear to tread, I do not claim to lay down the law about Russia, or to dogmatize about anything that has happened there. I have found the study of Soviet conditions an absorbing one" (pp. vii–viii).

Soviet Russia contains sixteen articles and a dozen photographs of Moscow, apparently included "at the insistence of the publisher," K. P. Dar of Allahabad Law Journal Press. In the first chapter, "Fascination of Russia," and the last chapter, "Russia and India," Jawaharlal examines India's need to understand and have good relations with the Soviet Union. In the second and third chapters, he briefly describes his journey from Berlin to Moscow, and his impressions of what he saw in the Russian capital. In the remaining chapters he comments on some aspects of the Soviet society, based mainly on his readings and reinforced by his personal contacts and visits during his short stay in Moscow, namely, the Soviet system of administration (4), salient features of the constitution of the U.S.S.R. (5), the place of the peasantry (9), administration of criminal law (10), the purpose of and the conditions in the prisons (11), the problems of minorities (12), the question of education (13), land reform (14), and the place of woman and marriage (15). There is a pen portrait of Lenin (7), and selected and annotated bibliography of books written from pro- and anti-Soviet points of view (6 and 8).

II *Fascination of Russia*

The chief interest in the book is Jawaharlal's fascination by Russia, and his realization in Moscow, after many imprisonments in India, that a closer relation between Russia and India might be of advantage to his country. Though he realized that reactions to the Russian phenomenon depended largely on the philosophy and outlook in life, goals, values and prejudices of the observer, he argues that the prudent course for Indians is not necessarily to follow the British line of denunciation of the revolutionary changes ushered in the Soviet Union. "No one can deny," he observes, "the fascination of this strange Eurasian country of hammer and sickle, where workers and peasants sit on the throne of the mighty and upset the best laid schemes of mice and men" (p. 4). Indians engaged in a freedom struggle to liberate their country from imperial Britain, and interested in its independent future, he felt, must seek more accurate picture of the gigantic changes taking place in their neighborhood for a number of reasons:

1. Though India had a marvelous civilization, it has suffered the present degradation and misery, partly because of her internal weaknesses which cannot be remedied by "vague fancies of our glorious past." In order to cope with the contemporary problems, India must seek "new avenues of thought and search for new methods" (p. 5).

2. Conditions and problems in pre-revolution Russia and British India are basically similar: imperial governments controlled and manipulated mainly for the benefit of a small group owning capital and land. Both countries are primarily agricultural, beginning to industrialize, with large problems of starving masses, illiteracy, landless peasantry, social injustices, and many minority communities. By means of the revolutionary changes, "if Russia finds a satisfactory solution for these problems," Jawaharlal argues, "our work in India is made easier" (p. 5).

3. Since contemporary Indian thinking about Soviet Russia is vigorously controlled by British-owned and subsidized news agencies inimical to Russia, Jawaharlal contends, in place of information, Indians are fed with "most fantastic stories, falsified reports allegedly by the Riga Correspondent," but actually written in London, and veiled propaganda to protect British economic interests. He gives four quotations from the New York *Nation* exposing the falsity of the "Riga Correspondent" (pp. 7–8). Without succumbing to such indoctrination, or inheriting this unwanted European rivalry between Britain and Russia, Jawaharlal argues, Indians should develop a pro-India policy rather than a pro-British Empire policy, towards the Soviet Union.

4. Russia is a geographical reality for India, being a neighbor, friendly or unfriendly, and a valid independent policy towards her, could only be based on accurate information, knowledge and understanding of the changes taking place there, and not on the basis of ignorance, propaganda or falsified accounts.

It is with this end in view that Jawaharlal proposes to give in his articles an objective appraisal of conditions in Russia, even though such views might be unpalatable to the British authorities and empire-supporting Indians. For he feels "we have to follow the line of life in its ever varying curves and avoid attempting to adhere rigidly to an outworn creed. At this early stage of his political life, Jawaharlal was beginning to project his historical perception in order to look at life afresh in every age, to be able to deal with contemporary problems.

III   *Visit to Moscow*

Whatever may have been Jawaharlal's impressions of his travel from Berlin to Moscow, and during his four days of stay in the Soviet capital, the actual reporting of such impressions some months later is all but too brief.[2] Nevertheless in the initial two chapters and in references scattered in others, he gives some glimpses of what he and his family experienced in this sojourn.

The Nehru family, including Jawaharlal's father, wife, and sister Krishna, left Berlin by train on November 6, passing through Poland whose countryside appeared to him rather "desolate and dismal," perhaps still carrying the signs of ravages of the 1914–18 war, or the dreary aspect may have been due to the approaching winter. But what appeared obvious to him was that "there were few evidences of industrialization." The train arrived in Niegeroloje, the Russian frontier town, on the night of November 7, after journeying for twenty-eight hours. There they were met by the Soviet state officials. After a small ceremony of welcome at the station, the visitors travelled further as state guests on a Russian train, and reached Moscow on the afternoon of November 8. Upon arrival in the Soviet capital, they were surprised to see "a number of Indian young men, including S. J. Saklatvala," among the officials awaiting them. The Nehrus were then taken to the Grand Hotel de Moscow in the Place de la Revolution where they were lodged for four days.

By the time the Nehrus arrived in Moscow, the main event of the celebration had already taken place the previous day. The more they heard accounts of it, the more they "regretted having missed this magnificent spectacle." However, from what he had heard, Jawaharlal recounted some of the main features of the celebration in his article:

> This consisted of a march past the Lenin mausoleum of over a million troops and workers and children drawn from every part of Russia. Kalinin, the peasant president of the Russian Union, and still a peasant in his appearance in spite of his high office, had taken the march past. From early morning till night had fallen the march past continued to the strains of the Internationale, the workers' anthem; first the troops of all kinds and then representatives from factories and colleges and schools, and towns and villages. Workers and peasants, men and women and children, forty deep went by, with banners flying, heads high and full of enthusiasm. Effigies there were of Chamberlain and Briand and Baldwin, some of them very clever. One of these showed Chamberlain wedged in a sickle with the hammer falling on his head. Finally, long after night had fallen the Cossack cavalry made a magnificent charge at break-neck speed right across the great Red Square. (pp. 15–16)

Jawaharlal records some vivid impressions of Moscow which then had a festive air with decorations, flags, and illuminations in red. "The red colour", he explains, "is dear to the Russians even apart from its revolutionary significance." In the Russian language, the word means both red color and being beautiful. Consequently, the famous old Red Square was red even before the revolution. "The first impression of Moscow," he writes, "is almost that of any great city" yet it stands apart from other cities of Western Europe, with its beautiful golden domes, wide squares, and a variety of costumes and headgears, mainly because of its Eurasian character. People were so accustomed to a variety of dress that they did not stare at other peoples' costumes as being eccentric or peculiar. "Even the saris of my wife and sister," he notes, "unusual as they were in Moscow, attracted less attention there than in Berlin or Paris." Another obvious difference was the absence of the contrast between extreme luxury and extreme poverty. Everywhere, whether he be "a porter at the railway station or a waiter in a restaurant, is a towerish 'comrade' and is addressed as such." Though big stores were state property, there were "small ones belonging to individuals," and even "street hawkers were trading in petty articles." While most of the people in the street were dressed regardless of fashion, "there were none of the dainties of the Rue de Rivoli or of Bond Street" (p. 22). He could not fail to notice some pre-revolutionary aspects of life surviving in the days of socialism, such as the Drosky, and begging in the streets. The officials explained that it was difficult to wean the beggars out from their age-long habit, though begging was much less prevalent than it used to be.

Among the places of interest they visited, Jawaharlal mentions Kremlin with its medieval wall, golden domes, Red Square, and Lenin Mausoleum. They paid a short visit to Kalinin, the President of the Union, who still looking like a peasant, lived simply "with no evidence of luxury or grandeur." They saw the Museum of Revolution, housed in the old English Club, and the former Nobles' Hall of Tsarist days converted into the Trade Union Hall. On a visit to the State Opera House, he noticed it was "overflowing with people in their work-a-day attire" without any attempt "at smartness or dressing up for the occasion."

Jawaharlal was much impressed by a revolutionary film they saw in a cinema theater. "The Last Days of Petrograd" showed the contrast between luxury and misery in the days of the Tsar, the struggle of the oppressed Russian people, ending in Lenin's victory. Jawaharlal who had suffered imprisonment in India on account of the freedom struggle was stirred by the heroic victory of the people and saw the immense propaganda value in the film for guiding the people towards revolutionary changes. "Though Russians are famous for the beauty and artistic excellence of their films," he laments, "unhappily we in India have no opportunity of seeing them." Instead, the Anglo-American cartels, by dumping their films in India were subjecting Indians "to gorgeous but stupid and inane productions," mainly to squeeze out enormous profits from the colony, while deadening the patriotic and revolutionary sensibilities of the people.

IV *Soviet Life and Society*

In discussing a number of aspects of Soviet life and society, Jawaharlal mentions his visits to some institutions in Moscow; among them are the Commissariat of Education, the Central Peasants Home, the Central Prison, and the Palace of Motherhood.

In spite of the official hostility of some of the West European and North American governments to the Soviets, Jawaharlal was surprised to find many professors, earnest students and inquirers, apart from tourists and businessmen from those countries, as well as many others, visiting Russia to study conditions on the spot. In the Commissariat of Education, the foreigners were learning about the educational system, agriculture, and cooperatives. There was "a high official of Afghan Ministry of Education, who was a student at Aligarh College in India" (p. 84). Yet the British Government prevented Indian educators and students from such visits and benefiting from the Russian experience. He hoped that universities in independent India would establish educational and cultural exchanges with Soviet institutions. The curriculum in Indian universities and their administrative structure was so rigged as to make them subservient to the British imperial purpose.

In recalling his visit to the Central Peasants Home, Jawaharlal mentions "the enormous building containing museums, demonstration rooms, lecture rooms and residential accommodation for about 350 persons. Practically everything that might interest or instruct the peasant was there" (p. 89). Another part of that building was devoted to health propaganda. Picture posters and models explained how disease was to be avoided and homes kept clean and healthy. Peasants from different parts of the Soviet Union were "encouraged to stay in the house for a maximum period of two months to go through a small course in agricultural training." He was told there were 350 such other centers throughout the Soviet Union. "Even one such center," Jawaharlal realized, "must improve the lot of the peasantry" (p. 90).

Jawaharlal who had learned to cherish freedom while studying law in England, and suffered the denial of that freedom in British India with long periods of residence in prisons, was naturally interested in the criminal law and prisons in the Soviet Union. Yet what Jawaharlal felt necessary was to understand the ideals which the Russians had placed before themselves, in order to examine the theory of the criminal law and what was considered a crime from the Soviet point of view, in contrast to the concept of crime in capitalistic, feudal, and imperial societies. Crime, according to soviet criminal law, is always the outcome of the antagonism existing in a society divided into classes; it is always the result of a faulty social organization and a bad environment (p. 102). Consequently, the 'punishment' has been replaced by a phrase, "measure of social defence." The convicts are subjected to collective work without complete deprivation of liberty. They cannot buy their way out by money since the "code lays down that in place of fine there can be no imprisonment, and no fine in place of imprisonment" (p. 106). The repressive measures, including death penalty are applied to "enemies of the people" and in case of "corruption and embezzlement of public funds", though the latter is a much condoned, lesser crime in feudal and capitalistic societies.

The prison which Jawaharlal visited was for the more serious offenders only, yet the prisoners wore no numbers nor special dress.[3] Upon his request he was taken to see two political prisoners, one a well-educated man and a good musician who "has been sentenced for ten years for spying in Russia on behalf of Czecho-Slovakia" (p. 113). Because of his skill he was made "the director of music in the jail." Though the visit to the prison was a short one, Jawaharlal realized that what was shown perhaps was "the brighter side of jail life." Yet it was, he found, an improvement over the old system prevailing in many countries. Jawaharlal was also conscious that the Soviet government had a special and ruthless way of treating its political opponents. Since such "counter-revolutionaries" and "enemies of the people" are betrayers of the society, the Soviet rulers found the humane principles of the general criminal law not applicable to them (p. 117).

Jawaharlal was much impressed by his visit to the Palace of Motherhood, containing "a fine exhibition of everything that relates to the health of the mother and the child." It carried on research, trained doctors, midwives, nurses, and sent out posters carrying messages to the distant villages, teaching "the father how to treat the mother, and the mother how to treat the baby, and both how to have a pleasant and clean home and healthy children" (p. 184). While legislating for women workers, the Soviets had given them though not necessarily equal, but special rights and privileges, particularly to those who were pregnant or nursing mothers; these were more progressive at that time than such rights and privileges in many other countries, e.g., four months of maternity vacation for industrial women workers, and three months for nonindustrial workers; nursing mothers allowed additional intervals, included in the working hours and paid for.

Jawaharlal's remaining articles do not represent his impressions of his visit but rather his studied approach to Soviet Russia, an approach motivated by his desire to understand her ways of tackling various human problems in a large country, such as education, peasantry and land distribution, the problem of minorities, etc. So also his two articles on the Soviet system and the constitution, are the result of his search for a constitution for independent India.

Jawaharlal sums up his final assessment of Soviet Russia as follows:

Russia has passed through ten years since the Bolshevik revolution. But it must be remembered that the first five of these ten years were entirely taken up in war against foreign and internal enemies and in the harder struggle against famine and blockade. A host of enemies attacked and tried to strangle her by cutting off her food supplies. For years the revolution hung in the balance and the economic life of the nation went to pieces. It is only during the past five years that she has had comparative peace and the chance to develop her resources. But even during this period she has had to contend against the hostility of most of the governments of Europe and of the super-capitalist United States of America. Having little money to develop her resources she has been denied credits and capital abroad. If she has progressed then during these five years it has been despite these difficulties. And the testimony of all competent observers is that she has progressed and has already made good the losses of the war period of eight years. (pp. 82–83)

When Jawaharlal left India in frustration as a congressman in 1926, he had already given up his childhood dream of an armed struggle to change the political situation in India. Gandhi had converted him to his ideology of nonviolent struggle as a Satyagrahi. Yet Jawaharlal was earnestly seeking a methodology which would facilitate the change of the political and economic structure of the country from the British colonial and Indian feudal institution to an independent, democratic, socialistic society. Beyond this primary concern for a means to an end, Jawaharlal's interest in the subtleties of doctrinaire socialism or virtues of communism were very luke-warm and noncommittal.[4] No doubt in his Cambridge days he had read about the West European ideologies of socialism and communism enunciated by a German Jew in the British capital. While in Moscow he saw the practical application of this West European ideology in an East European country, resulting in gigantic changes. But what he perhaps saw more clearly than ever before, during his second visit to Europe in 1926–27, first in Brussels, then in Berlin, and later in Moscow, was that to bring about all the political, social and economic changes in India and provide the many benefits to the masses, a reform within the British colonial system in the form of provincial autonomy, or even dominion status was not enough; complete independence from Britain was needed. It was this conviction that led Jawaharlal, upon his return to India in December 1927, to introduce at the Madras session of the Congress his famous epoch-making Complete Independence Resolution to the surprise of the Congress high command of that time, and almost challenging the authority of his father Motilal and his leader Gandhi.

CHAPTER 4

Letters: Letters From a Father to His Daughter (*1930*)

I *Juvenile Literature*

IN his second book Jawaharlal changed his style from journalism to letters, and contributed a charming little volume to children's literature. Combining his interest in science with paternal feelings, he sought to engage the curiosity of his ten-year-old child in his *Letters From a Father to His Daughter*. This novel treatment gives the dateless book an ever-fresh quality, and because of this, it may perhaps survive as Jawaharlal's sole literary creation among his other mass of historical writings.

The occasion for this series of letters was the time of separation of father and daughter in the summer of 1928. Jawaharlal was in Allahabad on the banks of Ganga attending to his work as the General Secretary of the Congress, while his daughter, Indira, was at a hill station Mussoorie in the Himalayas. Apparently, Jawaharlal sought to overcome the boredom of his political life by occasional escapes into quiet communion with his invisible daughter during the hot summer. For these letters have the resemblance of bedtime stories told by an indulgent father.

When some of Jawaharlal's friends suggested the publication of these letters, he felt they were too private and personal and were not intended for publication. Later when he agreed to do so, he was apparently motivated by his intense commitment to the promotion of his child-like dream of one-world society, and by the desire to share with others his aesthetic joy in the writing of his romance with scientific ideas. "I hope," he wrote in the foreword, that the readers of these letters may "gradually begin to think of this world of ours as a large family of nations" (a dream which crystallized two decades later in the United Nations), and that they may find in the reading of them "a fraction of the pleasure that I had in the writing of them."[1]

44   JAWAHARLAL NEHRU

The *Letters* was first published by Kitabistan of Allahabad in 1930 and was reprinted many times with numerous illustrations and photographs. Another edition of the *Letters* with color photographs was published by K. P. Dar at the Allahabad Law Journal Press in 1947. These letters have been translated and published in almost all the important languages of India, and in many languages abroad. In 1951 the book was published in the United States by John Day and Co., under a different title (as is often the case with U.S. publishers), namely, *The Story of the World*, containing one letter less than in the original, but including sketches by Richard Albany.

Though the title of the book suggests that the contents are letters, the text itself is in the form of distinct chapters, each with a chapter heading. There are no salutations or endings common to letters, nor is there any mention of dates and place names, as was done in the case of a later series of letters. Consequently, the book can be read merely as a juvenile story book, giving, as the subtitle indicates, "A Brief Account of the Early Days of the World Written for Children."

The book contains thirty-one letters. Jawaharlal starts his brisk narrative with vigor and enthusiasm, and relates the origin of the world in the solar system (1–3), the beginning of life on the earth and the evolution of man (4–6), emergence of different races and languages (7–10); the development of societies in an organized manner and the beginning of civilization (11–14). Though much of it is scientific speculation deduced from "discovered facts" such as fossils, the narrative does hold one's attention. Thereafter, Jawaharlal deals with the emergence of human societies in prehistoric times, basing his narrative mainly on social sciences. He states how group-leadership evolving from family patriarch, established the order of kings and nobles with power over other men (15–17); the beginnings of the centers of ancient civilization in Egypt and Crete, China and India (18–21); the nature of ancient international relations evolved through voyages and trade, and synthesizing of culture through languages, writings, and numerals (22–23); the division of labor and the growth of social institutions (24); organized religion and the priestcraft which claimed power over other men through the fear of the unknown (25). The next three chapters review the whole story and refer Indira to a number of picture post cards and photographs of fossils collected by the Nehru family (26–28). The last three chapters basically deal with the Indian situation, namely, "The Aryans came to India" (29); "What were the Aryans in India Like?" (30); and

"The *Ramayana* and the *Mahabharata*" (31). They were included in the collection because Jawaharlal felt at that time that "there is little chance of my adding to them" (p. ix). Little did he realize then that he was to write a longer series of letters two years later.

Though Jawaharlal commenced his correspondence with a view to give Indira a short account of "the story of our earth and the many countries, great and small, into which it is divided" (p. 1), in the process of telescoping millions of years in thirty-one letters, he did not go beyond the prehistoric period. The second part of his theme, namely, the story of many countries, great and small, or the story of the world during historic time of about 5,000 years, he developed in a second series of letters, written in prison two years later, and published under the title, *Glimpses of World History* (1934).

The reason for the sudden termination of the first series of letters was not a deliberate choice of the author but rather was caused by the changed political situation. At the end of the summer of 1928, Indira returned to Allahabad, and there was no Mussoorie or other hill station for her in the summer of 1929. Besides, Jawaharlal had hardly any time to continue a series of children's tales while he was engrossed with the burning political and social questions of the adult world. It was only when another prolonged separation of father and daughter was enforced upon them by his imprisonment during 1931 – 32, that Jawaharlal picked up the narrative once again. Thus, the abrupt ending of the first series of letters, happily clinches a short book of children's literature, leaving out the more detailed and complicated historical account of world history for the adult readers.

II   *Personalized Narrative*

Jawaharlal's choice of the subject for his correspondence would have ordinarily rendered the narrative to have the tone of a school teacher's dull account, presenting the reconstructed facts about prehistory. That it did not become so was mainly because of the author's special gifts in making his writing appealing to a little girl and hold her curiosity long enough. He achieved this by personalizing the narrative.

In the early chapters, Jawaharlal constantly refers Indira to her personal experiences of things seen and books read. By this process he keeps his writings within bounds of the little girl's comprehension. When he feels he has exhausted the treasure house of scientific facts, he scoops freely from social sciences in explaining the early tribal life and evolution of communities and nations, adding wit and humor here and there. At this point Jawaharlal realizes that perhaps his letters may not be interesting enough. "I am afraid," he apologizes in letter 15 that "my letters are getting a little complicated" for Indira to have continued interest (p. 44). The sense of endless wonder has to yield to matter of fact explanations about the beginnings of the complicated life. Yet Jawaharlal manages to capsule the story of the origin and growth of man, the evolution of human societies in such a manner as to help a young adult to understand the nature of accumulated conflicts in the modern world, and come to make intelligent decision on problems of contemporary life. He points out that we are today like "little children lost in a dark forest" (p. 44). Assuming a Virgilian mask, Jawaharlal proposes to lead his little daughter out of this wood of error to see clearly the ways in which men began in the earlier stages of civilization to appropriate property and power for personal gains causing endless inequalities on the one hand, and consequent struggle to restore a just equilibrium among people on the other, manifesting in the form of social changes or the socalled revolutions.

It is only when Jawaharlal comes to the end of his narrative in letter 26 that he asks his daughter the straightforward question: "Are you not tired of my letters!" (p. 73). Obviously, Jawaharlal was not able to gauge her immediate reactions to his letters which continued to explain his theory of the lost just society of noble savage, the Dharma Samsar, the Utopia or the Golden Age, through a lack of equitable restraint in human endeavors. It is in the magic of socialism, Jawaharlal assures the little girl that social justice could once again be achieved. By such dreamy political enchantment he was attempting to suspend Indira's disbelief and make her follow her father-guide to lead her out of the dark wood. After such a prophetic promise, Jawaharlal stops writing his epistolary entertainment. Thereafter he sends her some picture post cards and photographs from South Kensington Museum, hoping that they would be better than his "long and dull letters." He concludes the series by a definite suggestion that the romantic story of the prehistory has come to and end, "We have now finished our brief look back" (p. 97).

In this galloping sweep of a fairy-tale-like narrative, Jawaharlal was careful to include some touches of informality by introducing anecdotes from their family experiences in India and abroad, in order to make the pseudo-scientific mythology meaningful to a teenager. To suggest how man leaving the animal world became supreme by the power of his thought, he gives vivid imagery from Indira's experience in a gossipy manner: "you see today a little man sit on top of a great big elephant and make him do what he wills. The elephant is big and strong, far stronger than the little *mahaut* sitting on his neck. But the *mahaut* can think and because he can think he becomes the master and the elephant is his servant. So, as thought grew in man he became cleverer and wiser" (p. 5).

At other times, Jawaharlal draws on Indira's memories of their visits to places. For example, while discussing "What is life?" he refers her to Kew Gardens in London where he showed her the plants which "actually eat flies," or reminds her of "the gentleman who came to see us in Geneva," the Nobel Laureate, Jagadish Chandra Bose, who showed by experiments that not only plants have a great deal of life but also "he thinks that even stones have some life" (p. 10). Bose was improving upon the Upanishadic doctrine that "all that is, is Brahman," the unitary principle of the universe as creative energy. After reminding her of many fossils from the prehistoric period they had seen in many museums in London and Geneva, he tries to tell a convincing tale about the paleolithic man whose skull they had seen in Germany: "Do you remember going with us to see a professor in Heidelberg in Germany? He showed us a little museum full of fossils and specially an old skull which he kept carefully locked up in safe. This skull was supposed to belong to one of these earliest men. We now call him the Heidelberg man, simply because the skull was found buried near Heidelberg. Of course there was no Heidelberg or any other city in those days!" By injecting such anecdotes in his scientific story, Jawaharlal makes the letters delightful reading.

III   *Scientific Mythology*

Jawaharlal displays another remarkable gift—to weave romance with words in the process of mythologizing scientific ideas. The ancient art of fictionalizing fact is not lost in the scientist-historian. Myths in any culture embody human experiences explaining rightly or wrongly that which is not easily comprehended. Thus mankind acts and lives on the basis of some basic or fundamental myths. It is only when myths of one age are no longer the driving dreams of another, that one could see how absurd some of these myths were. Even some of our recent myths, such as the "mission to civilize the world," or the "white man's burden," or "superior race," "*uber alles*," "chosen people," are losing their force. But the myths of a few centuries earlier, such as those that produced the crusades, the inquisition, jehad or holy wars of all kinds for the assertion of the superiority of one race, ideology, or institution—all these appear like ridiculous farces after a time when people have ceased to believe in them.

On the other hand, some of the culture myths have come down through the transmitting traditions, and continue to be a part of our living experiences. Since they contain man's approximations to understand the unknown, they peal off layers of meaning, depending upon the manner in which they are interpreted. For example, the myths about the primeaval mating and creation, be it a Vedic myth of Diti and Aditi (Finite and Infinite), or the Semitic myth of Adam and Eve (the first man, and the breath of life in woman), or the Taoist myth of Yin and Yang (Earth and Heaven), or Ilmatar's seven hundred years of pregnancy on the water bed, all these myths have the peculiar quality of satisfying man's endless need to explain the unexplainable. Such culture myths and racial memories when sanctified become transmitted from age to age as "religious realities."

In his *Letters* Jawaharlal casts aside all the traditional culture myths about creation. Instead, he freely recreates from contemporary science journalism "scientific myths" about the origin of the world, evolution of life on the earth, coming of man from the animal world, and the growth of human society in prehistoric times. These scientific myths (unlike the culture myths capsuled out of tribal and racial memories), are based on rational explanations deduced from evidence gathered through natural and social sciences and internationally accepted. If the children of the world are to be indoctrinated about some myths, Jawaharlal seems to hold, it would be better for them to be exposed to a common stock of scientific mythology than to subject them to conflicting and contradictory culture myths. He expects the children to believe in these science myths mainly because they satisfy in some way the thinking of average science-oriented twentieth-century adult mind. In this mythical sense, Jawaharlal may be regarded as a natural *rishi* writing a prose science *Purana*.

For the purpose of telling the story of the world to a modern young child, Jawaharlal argues, the only book or scripture worth examining is what he calls, "The Book of Nature." "We have rocks and mountains and seas," he writes, "and stars and rivers and deserts and fossils of old animals. These and other like things are our books for the earth's early story" (p. 2). Such facts of nature that are around us all the time, Jawaharlal thinks, tell us something more near the truth than "the most beautiful fairy tales" imagined by men in different cultures at different times in history, trying to relate the tale of creation.

For Jawaharlal the method of studying the Book of Nature is like studying any other book. First one learns the alphabet of the language and then masters the language itself. Once one masters the alphabet and the language of the Book of Nature, one can unlock many of nature's mysteries and the story of creation of earth will unfold itself like an open sesame. This study essentially is in the spirit of scientific inquiry and includes in the first instance, all natural sciences and secondarily social sciences and humanities. Fortunately, Jawaharlal tells us that "scientists and those who have studied and thought a great deal about these matters" together give us a great deal of the story of the earth, and one could accept their testimony (p. 1). On the other hand, he tells his daughter, since the Book of Nature is an open book, it is equally open for any one with free imagination to inquire into the story of the earth as easily as a scientist does, and gives an example:

If you see a little round shiny pebble, does it not tell you something? How did it get round and smooth and shiny without any corners or rough edges? If you break a big rock into small bits, each bit is rough and has corners and rough edges. It is not at all like a round smooth pebble. How then did the pebble become so round and smooth and shiny? It will tell you its story if you have good eyes to see and ears to hear it. It tells you that once upon a time, it may be long ago, it was a bit of a rock, just like the bit you may break from a big rock or stone with plenty of edges and corners. Probably it rested on some mountain side. Then came the rain and washed it down to the little valley where it found a mountain stream which pushed it on and on till it reached a little river. And the little river took it to the big river. And all the while it rolled at the bottom of the river and its edges were worn away and its rough surface made smooth and shiny. So it became the pebble that you see. Somehow the river left it behind and you found it. If the river had carried it on, it would have become smaller and smaller till at last it became a grain of sand and joined its brothers at the seaside to make a beautiful beach where little children can play and make castles out of the sand. (pp. 2–3).

Thus Jawaharlal's 'scientific fact' becomes somewhat mythologized in the version of the storyteller. What we have here basically is a continuing contest between Jawaharlal the student of science and

Jawaharlal the lover of art who wants to tell a story; Jawaharlal born within the Indian tradition of Puranic fiction, and Jawaharlal whose mental make-up was conditioned by the early twentieth-century European rationalism. Yet in his letters, Jawaharlal the scientist is overcome by Jawaharlal the writer and that inspite of himself. For the spirit of free inquiry is overtaken by the spirit of freer imagination, and in that romance of ideas, Jawaharlal carries his ten-year-old daughter across eons of time. Nothing could be farther from the scientific spirit than the imaginative recreation of the epic of the shiny pebble without being unable to resist that urge to resort to the literary device of "once upon a time"!

As a consequence of Jawaharlal's ready acceptance of the scientific hypothesis about the creation of the world and life in it, he was able to liberate himself from the historical tradition and see some of the culture myths as myths. For example, the traditional Indian attitudes to creation—innumerable as they are, be they of polytheism, henotheism, monotheism, or monism, deriving from the Vedas and the Upanishads, or the classical Indian trinity of Brahma the creator, Vishnu the preserver, and Siva the destroyer, or the Puranic myths about creation—all these are completely dismissed. On the other hand, he accepts the theory of the stellar universe, a postulation of modern astrophysics as a fact, and the theory of evolution as the real process. The anthropomorphic "god" or "gods" as agency of creation have no place in his science mythology. Such a creator myth is too stale and sterile and out-dated concept to be told to a child of ten in the twentieth century. The tribal explanation and religious myth based on racial lines have been deflated and cast aside.

The question that arises is: can a child believe in a scientific fact such as the "million years in the making of the earth"? Even adult minds seem to lose grip of this scientific fact, or such other facts as the "boundless space" or the "unnumbered earthly years" which perhaps mean little or nothing outside the confines of our planet. Jawaharlal seems to think otherwise. He credits human imagination with power to encompass any myth indoctrinated to children to make meaning; so why not indoctrinate them with myths that would create uniformity of approach among children of the world in all cultures and regions so that they may grow up to be children of one large family with a common science mythology, rather than be enslaved and terrorized by tribal myths of different cultures. Jawaharlal's simple solution for the mental adjustment and reintegration of human personality seems to be very much rooted in Buddha's saying: "All that we are is the result of our thinking,"[2] a dictum which the UNESCO has adopted in the preamble of its charter. Jawaharlal's one-world society, therefore, begins as a concept in the minds of children of the world based on the common fund of science mythology.

What then is Jawaharlal trying to do in his letters to his daughter? Apart from the entertainment aspect, with his geophysical frame of mind and scientific attitudes, he is overstepping on the past cultural history, and advocating a new mode of awakening young people's minds to an acceptable story of the world in which the tribal god of a group of people did not create it all; that the earth is but a cast-off piece from the burning sun (p. 8); and "belongs to the family of the sun, the solar system"; that the sun itself is but a small star in the unknown stellar universe (pp. 7–8); that the romantic moon (now not so romantic since the cosmonauts and astronauts, belonging to earthly rival tribes have examined it closely) is no more than a lump of earth cast aside in the like manner, probably from the region of the Pacific Ocean (p. 8); that all forms of life on earth gradually evolved from amoeba (p. 12). Consequently, all the accounts of laborious creation mentioned in the "churning of the Ocean of Milk" familiar to the Indian imagination, the various accounts of Mesopotamian Jehova's six-day tight work schedule familiar to the Sumerians, Semitics in the Judaic-Christian-Islamic mythology, or any other mythical account of earlier tribes in any other regions, are, from Jawaharlal's point of view, stale myths as the fabulous legends about the rainbow, or the flatness of the earth, or the man in the moon!

Letters from a Father to His Daughter is the first of its kind in the body of Indo-English literature, or for that matter, in the whole of Indian literary tradition. It is quite possible that Jawaharlal may have read Oliver Goldsmith's series of letters, *The Citizen of the World*. But it is obvious that he was familiar with the science fiction of his time, especially works of H. G. Wells. He often found expressions from *Alice in the Wonderland* to explain his own life situation becoming "curioser and curioser." Jawaharlal may have unconsciously felt like imitating Lewis Carroll's technique of telling a wonderful story to a little girl; however his story is not about a Mr. Rabbit but a rabbit-like thing racing in space in the stellar universe, the little Mr. Earth.

CHAPTER 5

World View:
Glimpses of World History (*1934*)

I *Prison Literature*

JAWAHARLAL'S major works were all written while he was imprisoned by the British government. When he was outside the prison, he was too much occupied with the work of the Indian National Congress and the freedom struggle. Though he issued statements, made speeches, and wrote reports during that time, his energies were taken up, for the most part, by his active life. In the prison, on the other hand, in spite of physical discomfort and hardships of all kinds often resulting in ill-health, Jawaharlal could only resort to intense intellectual exercises. In such a state of expanded mental horizon, he examined past and present events, their causes and consequences—or the cumulative social, national, and international karma—and synthesizing them in a meaningful way related them to the world in which he lived. While in prison, he also came to realize that "a period in prison is a very desirable part of one's education."[1] A period of exile or isolation has been traditionally considered as a way of *tapas*, and most of the Indian epic heroes had benefited by such discipline.

Out of his self-examination within the prison walls, Jawaharlal produced, besides occasional writings, three outstanding works upon which his fame as a writer mainly rests. These classics of prison literature are: *Glimpses of World History*, *An Autobiography*, and *The Discovery of India*. Though all these three works are basically historical works, they are intensely personal, and together present Jawaharlal's philosophy of history and his world view.

Jawaharlal assures the readers that "there have been many famous literary gaol-birds" and that he has been keeping respectable company among similarly placed men of letters of the past (p. 950). Dante in his exile had to descend into limbo in order to find his place among five other great poets of ancient Greece and Rome. But for Jawaharlal past is a living present and is continuous in the future. So he could recall these men who, instead of despairing in the prison, saw glimpses of the truth in their own particular fields of investigation. Ssu-ma Ch'ien (145–86 B.C.), the Grand Historian of Han Dynasty of China and the creator of *Shih chi* (Historical Records); Ibn Khaldun of Tunis (1332–1406), the Arab historian and author of *The Muqaddimah (An Introduction to History)*; Hugo Grotius (1583–1645), the Dutch Jurist who wrote *De Jura Belli et Pacis (Rights of War and Peace)*; Miguel de Cervantes (1547–1616), the gallant Spaniard who saw the grand vision of *Don Quixote de la Mancha*; and John Bunyan (1628–1688), the stubborn nonconformist, whom the British government imprisoned to expiate his crime of conscience! Yet Jawaharlal knew that he was a different kind of prisoner, for he had declared in 1922 when he was arrested for nonviolent demonstration: "We go to prison to absorb the evil of our oppressors and thereby redeem them." Consequently, among all the past literary "gaol-birds," Jawaharlal was one of the few who chose the prison, like Socrates, believing in the justness of his cause and with a view to rectify the unjust law by which the society was ruled. Because of this, he felt the triumph of the spirit even when he was enclosed by prison walls. This fearless freedom gave him a unique point of view from which to view himself and the outside world in his works.

II *Further Letters*

Jawaharlal wrote *Glimpses* in three prisons during 1930–33, with eleven months interval in between. The introductory birthday letter to Indira, dated October 26, 1930, and the first eighteen letters, were written in Naini prison when he was imprisoned for the fifth time, for taking part in the no-tax campaign as a part of the Non-Cooperation and Civil Disobedience Movement launched by the Congress under Gandhi's leadership. Jawaharlal was arrested on October 19, in Allahabad, tried in Naini prison, and sentenced on October 29 for two years rigorous imprisonment and a fine of 600 rupees. He was released on January 26, 1931, along with other Congress leaders, in an attempt by the British to come to terms with the Congress, which resulted in the Gandhi–Irwin Pact of March 1931.

Jawaharlal wrote two more letters (19 and 20, dated April 21 and 22, 1931), on board the *S.S. Cracovia* on the Arabian Sea while sailing from Bombay to Colombo. He was going for a holiday to Ceylon with Kamala, in order to recuperate from the ill-health he had suffered in the prison.

The remaining 176 letters (21–196), were written in two prisons when Jawaharlal was imprisoned for the sixth time under framed charges. Gandhi had reluctantly attended the second session of the doomed round-table conferences in London. When the news came of its failure, the British felt insecure in India and feared the Civil Disobedience Movement would plague them once again. Jawaharlal was on his way to Bombay to meet Gandhi who was due to return from London two days later. To prevent that meeting, the British government arrested him in Delhi on December 26, 1930, tried him in prison, as was usual under the colonial rule, and sentenced him to two years rigorous imprisonment and a fine of 500 rupees. After six weeks in Naini prison, he was transferred to Bareilly District Gaol where he was detained for four months. During that time he wrote thirty-five letters (21–55). Thereafter, he was transferred to Dehra Dun Gaol, where he was kept without a break for the rest of his sentence, until he was released on August 30, 1933. Jawaharlal wrote the remaining 141 letters (56–196) in Dehra Dun Gaol. All these letters in this series are dated and carry a title.

Just a few days prior to his release, Jawaharlal was pleasantly surprised by "a mountain of letters" he had written to his daughter, and wondered whether all that effort, paper, and ink were worth expending. He was not sure whether or not they conveyed any message of interest to Indira. Yet he felt that his labor of love in the prison was worth his while. "Whether you care for them or not," Jawaharlal wrote in his last letter, "you cannot grudge me the joy of having written them, day after day during those two long years. It was winter when I came. Winter gave place to our brief spring, slain all too soon by the summer heat, and then, when the ground was parched and dry and men and beasts panted for breath, came the monsoon, with its bountiful supply of fresh and cool rainwater. Autumn followed, and the sky was wonderfully clear and blue and the afternoons were pleasant. The year's cycle was over, and again it began: winter and spring and summer and the rainy season. I have sat here, writing to you and thinking of you, and watched the seasons go by" (p. 949).

After his release, Jawaharlal collected all the letters and wrote a preface dated January 4, 1934, without knowing "when or where these letters will be published, or whether they will be published at all" (p. vii). But he wanted to put them aside when he still had the time to do so, before he got lost once again in India's freedom struggle, or imprisoned. That same year the letters were published in two volumes by Kitabistan of Allahabad under the title *Glimpses of World History*. The publication of this unusual book on history ushered Jawaharlal the writer on the world literary scene. Subsequently, at the request of the publisher, Jawaharlal added a postscript dated Arabian Sea, November 14, 1938, while he was sailing for Europe. The revised and up-to-date edition in one volume, containing about a thousand pages, was published by Lindsay Drummon Ltd. in London and by Kitabistan. This edition also contains fifty maps by J. F. Horrabin who had also illustrated H. G. Wells' *Outlines of History*. Some of the illustrations are identical.

In the United States, the *Glimpses of World History* was published in 1942 by John Day Co., which also published an abridged version in 1960 under the title *Nehru on World History*, containing excerpts from fifty-three letters. The editor, Saul K. Padover, states that the guiding principle of his condensation was, "the universality of interest combined with unconventionality of interpretation." Obviously he was fascinated by Jawaharlal's "grand sweep of history," particularly where he indulges "in philosophic reflections and trenchant generalizations." Padover considered Jawaharlal's *Glimpses* as "a philosophy of history illustrated by certain broad aspects of the record of humanity."[2]

III *Personal Letters*

The letters included in the *Glimpses* are all not necessarily on history. Some of them are personal and most others have intimate and personal references meant only for Indira. After his release from the prison, Jawaharlal thought of separating them but he realized that it was not easy to take them out without considerable effort, and for that reason he left them untouched in the collection (p. vii). Among them are the introductory birthday letter and eight others.[3] These letters and other personal references scattered in other letters enliven the historical material in the book, just as Dante's physical presence is made meaningful among the non-living in the long journey. This invisible presence of the author as a character in his work raises the *Glimpses of World History* to epic proportion, reminding the readers of Valmiki's presence in the *Ramayana* or *Vyasa's* presence in the *Mahabharata*. The technique of narration in which a father transmits his thoughts to his daughter somewhat resembles the format of the Indian epics wherein an older sage recites his work to a younger disciple. The autobiographical element in the book, thus serves two purposes: running like a golden thread, it holds the multi-patterned fabric of the historical story together, and it makes a pleasant reading because of the spirit of robust humanism of the author injected into it.

If Jawaharlal's first series of *Letters* in which he used scientific mythology to tell the prehistoric story of the world is regarded as a mini-science *Purana*, then his second series of further letters, giving accounts of the story of the earth and of the many countries, great and small, in which it is divided during the historic time, can be considered *Ithihasa*. The remembrance of things past gives a panoramic vision of the rise and fall of human civilizations on the face of the earth. In this creative process, Jawaharlal lives through a personal and national epic struggle to be free from bondage, and drags his little daughter along on the way to be a witness to a Satyagrahi's pilgrim's progress.

The opening letter in the *Glimpses*, dated Central Prison, Naini, October 26, 1930, is addressed to "Indira Priyadarshini on her Thirteenth Birthday."[4] In it Jawaharlal wonders what present he could send her from a prison. "My presents cannot be very material or solid," he wrote trying to overcome his situation. "They can only be of the air and of the mind and spirit—things that even the high walls of prison cannot stop" (p. 1). These non-material presents, he explains to his daughter, enrich a person differently, inasmuch as a person becomes like a lighted lamp lighting another. Such presents the Mahatma is distributing liberally to ordinary men and women in the country, who in spite of their not being ordinarily heroic in nature, have risen to be heroes in the freedom struggle. When a great leader inspires a whole nation, and makes them do great deeds, then "history becomes stirring and epoch making." By communicating to Indira this spirit of brave deeds (about which he had dreamt in his school days) as a birthday present, Jawaharlal assures the little girl that she is "fortunate in being a witness to this great struggle," and almost prophetically assures her that she would "grow up into a brave soldier in India's service" (p. 3).

Two months later, Jawaharlal continues his series of further letters on New Year's Day 1931. In the first three letters he sets the basic premise for his heroic undertaking. He feels that the history of the world cannot be understood in terms of fragmented history of a nation which is only a small part in the family of nations. For a comprehensive world history from the global point of view, one would require a great deal of effort and library of scholarship to write it. Realizing this problem, and also the fact that he was thoroughly unequipped, Jawaharlal outlines his project: "I cannot write for you the history of my choice. You will have to go to other books for it. But I shall write to you from time to time something about the past and about the people who lived in the days gone by, and who played a big part on the world's stage" (p. 5).

In making this undertaking, Jawaharlal was conscious that history was not something past to be studied, but that it was in fact a living present. It was a stage on which many men and women have acted their parts and gone, and that stage is still open for others, and he is on that stage too. "To read history is good," he wrote, "but even more interesting and fascinating is to help in making history" (p. 4). Whether he was inside the prison or outside, he felt, he was participating in the crowded moments of history. Yet the historic decision to write about history was not made for historical reasons but to overcome the separation enforced upon Indira and her parents who were kept apart from each other in two different prisons by an unfriendly foreign government:

> You must be rather lonely. Once a fortnight you may see Mummie, and once a fortnight you may see me, and you will carry our messages to each other. But I shall sit down with pen and paper and I shall think of you. And then you will silently come near me and we shall talk of many things. And we shall dream of the past, and find our way to make the future greater than the past. So on this New Year's Day let us resolve that, by the time this year also grows old and dies, we shall have brought this bright future dream of ours nearer to the present, and given to India's past a shining page of history. (p. 5)

Like the supreme confidence in the poetic vision in which young Shakespeare and aged Valmiki declared to the world that "as long as men can breathe and eyes can see," and "as long as rivers continue to flow on the earth," their works will live among mankind, so also Jawaharlal sees in the prison cell not the dull monotony enclosed by brick walls, but the assurance of a glorious page in history.

By the time Jawaharlal had written eighteen letters, he was released from the prison. Thereafter, he was involved more in the
making of history than writing about it. In letters 19 and 20, written
on board *S.S. Cracovia* he recalls the gap of three months since he
wrote his last letter. He was again detached and isolated from the
Indian political situation and could engage in a stream of consciousness like reflection wherein time and geography lost their barriers.
During these three months he was out of prison, Motilal had died,
and the Congress had suspended Satyagraha on account of the ill-
conceived and unsatisfactory Gandhi-Irwin Pact. Though he was
free and was going on a holiday to Ceylon, "What is our freedom
worth if India is not free?" he asks (p. 54). Yet these great changes in
the family and in the nation, he felt, were all insignificant in the
reckoning of ages. "Three months of Change!" Jawaharlal wrote as
if challenging history, "A drop in the ocean of time, a bare second in
the life of a nation! Only three weeks ago I went to see the ruins of
Mohenjo Daro in the Indus Valley!" (p. 55). How long ago was it
that people lived there in their glory? No one remembers. Only their
memories survive, and "sometimes in our dreams and reveries we
imagine ourselves back in those times and doing brave deeds like the
heroes and heroines of the old" (p. 2). Thus Jawaharlal changes the
scale of his vision from personal to the historical and wades through
the *maya* declaring that "when one takes the unreal to be the real,
the real becomes unreal."

It did not take long for the British government to imprison
Jawaharlal once again for the sixth time after an interval of eleven
months. In letter 21, dated March 26, 1932, written in Bareilly District Gaol, he resumed his letter-sequence. "Fourteen months have
passed," he wrote, "since I wrote to you from Naini Prison about
past history." While rooted in the prison cell, his mind wandered
recalling his journey to Ceylon, the sights he had seen in ancient
Lanka, and their voyage northwards through south India from
Kanyakumari to Prayag. He also realized that it had taken three
months of solitary confinement to bring him back to his old historical narrative and that return was not easy. "I have taken long in
resuming these letters to you," he wrote apologetically, "but you
know how difficult it is sometimes to think of the distant past when
the present fills the mind. It takes some little time for me to settle
down in gaol and to avoid worrying about happenings outside. I
shall try to write to you regularly" (p. 57).

Thereafter Jawaharlal's letters flowed in a continuous stream except for a break in letter 56, when he was transferred from Bareilly Gaol to Dehra Dun Gaol. By then his enthusiasm for his story had begun to lag. "I remember the promise I made to you, and I shall try to fulfill it," he assures her. "But more even than this is the joy that the thought of you gives me when I sit down to write and imagine that you are by me and we are talking to each other" (p. 172).

When another New Year's Day came by, Jawaharlal recalled in letter 120, "It is my third consecutive New Year's Day in prison." During the last eleven years he had the singular misfortune, thanks to the British government, to spend five New Year's Days in prison, and wondered, "how many more such days and other days I shall see in prison?" Yet as history was in the making, he felt like "a vegetable rooted to one place." He realized that "one gets used to everything in time, even to the routine and sameness of gaol." In such a state of prolonged, isolated, and imprisoned life what did a long series of letters mean to the writer?

> They may be dull reading to you and tedious and prolix. But they have filled up my gaol life and given me an occupation which has brought me a great deal of joy. It was just two years ago today on New Year's Day that I began them in Naini Prison, and I continued them on my return to gaol. Sometimes, I have not written for weeks, sometimes I have written daily. When the mood to write captured me and I sat down with pen and paper, I moved in a different world, and you were my darling companion and gaol with all its work was forgotten. These letters thus came to represent for me my escapes from gaol. (p. 476)

In spite of his long imprisonments and the hardships imposed on him and his family, Jawaharlal did not despair. "We have the joy of working and struggling for a great cause," he wrote. "We have a great leader, a beloved friend and a trusty guide whose sight gives strength and whose touch inspires; and we have the surety that success awaits us, and sooner or later we shall achieve it" (p. 477). This faith in the cause for which he was suffering, gave him the strength to endure the hardships.

In his last letter, dated August 19, 1933, Jawaharlal definitely concludes his long series: "We have finished, my dear; the long story has ended" (p. 949). But the desire to finish off with a flourish induced him to set down his final personal thoughts about his letters as if they constituted his personal philosophy of history:

> Indeed, all that we have today of culture, civilization, science, or knowledge of some aspects of the truth, is a gift of the distant or recent past to us. It is right that we acknowledge our obligation to the past. But the past does not

exhaust our duty or obligation. We owe a duty to the future also, and perhaps that obligation is even greater than the one we owe to the past. For the past is past and done with, we cannot change it; the future is yet to come, and perhaps we may be able to shape it a little. If the past has given us some part of the truth, the future also hides many aspects of the truth, and invites us to search for them. But often the past is jealous of the future and holds us in a terrible grip, and we have to struggle with it to get free to face and advance towards the future. (pp. 951–52)

It was with this realization of the gifts of the past and a higher duty to the future, and after a *tapas* in the prison that Jawaharlal felt the call to action very refreshing. Quoting Romain Rolland, "Action is the end of thought," Jawaharlal explained: since he was servant to thought for so long, now it was time for him to be servant to action, and not to escape action for fear of its consequences. In this spirit of adventure, he concluded that people everywhere have clearly a choice for action in spite of governmental or institutional oppression. The choice some men have is to go up the mountain and see the light, and then coming down to the valley to transmit that light to others, thus fulfilling, in Buddha's words, the obligations of the enlightened and the awakened: "All of us have our choices of living in the valleys below with their unhealthy mists and fogs, but giving a measure of bodily security; or of climbing the high mountains, with risk and danger for companions, to breathe the pure air above, and take joy in the distant views, and welcome the rising sun" (p. 953).

In this tone of high idealism and human adventure, Jawaharlal concludes his last letter with a quotation from Tagore's Nobel Prize winning *Gitanjali*, "Where the mind is without fear and the head is held high," hoping that mankind, including Indians and their oppressors the British, would progress towards perfection, an ideal human society, the *dharma samsara*, which is not "broken up into fragments by narrow domestic walls."[5]

Through these personal letters and personal references in others, Jawaharlal infuses the dead bones of history with autobiographical lyricism and makes his letters come to life. Indira, the "Glimpse of Love" (Priyadarshini), no doubt remains Jawaharlal's Beatrice, helping him to escape the Inferno into which the British had cast him; yet the very human voyager has with him another source of strength, the strength of his profound faith in the great cause to which he was committed, and the greatness of the cause lifts him above the ordinary and sustains him.

IV   *Visions of History*

The *Glimpses*, no doubt, has much more adult material on history than a young girl of thirteen or fourteen years could grasp. Jawaharlal suggests that if Indira were to find it at all difficult to follow, then she should "skip those parts," for he admits that perhaps "the grown-up in me got the better of me sometimes" (p. 950). That much apology he tenders to his daughter for not remaining strictly within the confines of juvenile literature as he did in his earlier work, *Letters from a Father to His Daughter*.

Yet the *Glimpses* are not mere juvenile platitudes. There are shrewd observations on human nature and astute generalizations on human action which the grownups could find to be surprisingly clear. However, he was conscious that he was not writing history but conversing about it unhurriedly in a selective manner, that too in the privacy of his cell with his invisible daughter. This eerie quality about these letters makes them truly glimpses of the greatest continuous show on earth, the story of man. "You must not take," he warns his daughter, "what I have written in these letters as the final authority on any subject. A politician wants to have a say on every subject, and he always pretends to know much more than he actually does" (p. 950). With that honest statement perhaps Jawaharlal sought to disarm not only his daughter's disbelief, but also his would-be critics before their attack was even planned.

Self-conscious self-analysis has been Jawaharlal's special gift as evidenced from his *Autobiography* as well as from the devastatingly clear-cut letter he wrote to the press about himself under the pseudonym of "Chanakya" prior to his own re-election as the president of the Congress in 1937.[6] That same frank admission of his own weaknesses in writing accounts of world history easily comes through in Jawaharlal's final letter:

These letters of mine are but superficial sketches joined together by a thin thread. I have rambled on, skipping centuries and many important happenings, and then pitching my tent for quite a long time on some event which interested me. As you will notice, my likes and dislikes are pretty obvious, and so also sometimes are my moods in gaol. I do not want you to take all this for granted; There may, indeed, be many errors in my accounts. A prison, with no libraries or reference books at hand, is not the most suitable place in which to write on historical subjects. I have to rely very largely on the many note-books which I have accumulated since I began my visit to gaol twelve years ago. Many books have also come to me here; they have come and gone, for I could not collect a library here. I have shamelessly taken from these books facts and ideas; there is nothing original in what I have written. (p. 950)

What is special, then, about the *Glimpses*, if it is not history and if it is not original, especially if the subject matter is to be found in many books which are available to any reader? Jawaharlal's book perhaps has the abiding interest because of its unconventional approach to history and the manner in which he highlights elements of human interest in the story of the world. Appropriately, he does not call his work an "outline" or "introduction" to world history but simply "glimpses" of world history. The subject matter of his glimpses is a thing apart, and is left to professional historians. It is they who devoting their lifetime, meticulously record, collate, examine and relate the facts and other raw material of history, and then deduce whatever generalizations they may from their own light or darkness. Being not a historian by training or profession, he does not claim to usurp their place. But he is willing to use the fruits of their labors. He is not a historian, but he sees irresistible enchantment in observing the majestic march of historical events. "If you look upon past history with the eye of sympathy," he writes, "the dry bones will fill up with flesh and blood, and you will see a mighty procession of living men and women and children in every age and every clime, different from us and yet very like us, with much the same human virtues and human failings. History is not a magic show, but there is plenty of magic in it for those who have eyes to see" (p. 951).

It was what he "saw" in history that he recorded in *Glimpses*. Yet what he saw was perhaps conditioned by the Indian philosophic attitude embodied in the principle of *darsana* in which the sages maintained that truth becomes revealed in intuitive apprehensions in the experiencing of the macrocosm in the microcosm.[7] For truth itself escapes man's perception and rationality, and what is packaged in concepts and language is not the truth, but some aspects of it. Consequently the truth of history, in spite of many aspects of it being laboriously recorded in languages and interpreted in books, man could come to understand through realization of the meaning of the cycles of civilization and the waves of historical movements in momentary *darsana* or in "glimpses". Jawaharlal found this effort worthwhile in order to become aware of one's own place in the historical sweep of events. To understand another age, to comprehend the rhythm in the rise and fall of empires and civilizations, the growth and decay of institutions, the unceasing conflict of ever-changing attitudes and unchanging ideas, and the continuous movement forward, as Krishna said to Arjuna in life's battlefield of Kurukshetra—all these have to be viewed and related in the proper perspective, and for this purpose Jawaharlal took a unique point of view, nonreligious, nondogmatic, and nondoctrinaire, and considerably less ethnocentric than most previous writers.

The manner of arriving at the glimpses of history, Jawaharlal maintains, is for one to look upon history with sympathy and with understanding. "To understand a person who lived long ago, you will have to understand his environment, the conditions under which he lived, the ideas that filled his mind. It is absurd for us to judge past people as if they lived now and thought as we do . . . We cannot judge the past from the standards of the present. Every one will willingly admit this. But everyone will not admit the equally absurd habit of judging the present by the standards of the past. The various religions have especially helped in petrifying old beliefs and faiths and customs, which may have had some use in the age and country of their birth, but which are singularly unsuitable in our present age" (p. 950–51).

Some characteristics of Jawaharlal's unconventionality become obvious even while glancing at the headings of his letters. For example, "The Burden of Old Tradition" (9); "A Famous Conqueror but a Conceited Young Man," referring to Alexander of Macedonia, whom Dante regarding as a butcher boiled in blood in the Seventh Circle of Inferno (17); "The Roman Empire Splits Up and Finally Becomes a Ghost" with an implied suggestion that British Empire too is on its way out (33); "Hindu Imperialism under the Guptas" to remind Indians of the nature of imperialism (37); "The Roman Church Becomes Militant" thus destroying the very basis for its existence under the teaching of Jesus (70); "Europe Begins to Grab in East Asia" (79); "England Cuts Off the Head of Her King" (87); "The Coming of the Big Machine" (97); "The Invisible Empire of America" (138); "Seven Hundred Years Conflict Between Ireland and England" (139); "Turkey Becomes the 'Sick Man of Europe'" (142); "What Independence Means under the British" in Egypt (164); "Iraq and the Virtues of Aerial Bombing" over the so-called 'trust territory' (169); "The Strange Behaviour of Money" (173). Jawaharlal's buoyant spirit is chuckling under these comic captions at the vanity of human ambition, in the manner of Honoré de Balzac, Dante, or Wu Cheng-en. There is also a good deal of satire implied in the way historical actions are presented, a satire that is not literally condemnatory but charmingly good-natured. The sense of the comic adds to the unconventionality of the approach.

Another feature of Jawaharlal's unconventionality is the shift in his point of view. Traditionally history has been viewed from the ethnocentric point of view of the writer—be he Chinese, Arab, Greek, European or American. Writers viewed "world history" from their national or regional point of view. "World" in this sense meant the limits of their known experience and not necessarily the global context and all the continents in it. The world of Utnapistim or Noah was essentially the world of their experience in the Mesopotamian valley. The world civilization for the Chinese was the dominions of the "universal emperor" or the "son of heaven," who exercised his sway mainly in East Asia. Alexander conquered the world that was known to the Greeks, that is, the Persian Empire and the countries surrounding the Mediterranean. Ibn Khaldun's *Universal History* records details of Arab hegemony in Southwest Asia and North Africa and does not extend to Mars. European and American "world history" invariably begins with Greek and Hebrew culture, with some footnotes on India and China. Even H. G. Wells' *Outlines of History of Mankind* deals mainly with the growth and expansion of European civilization arising from Greco-Semitic roots, with a charitable, somewhat peripheral, consideration of Asia.

Jawaharlal shifts this Europe-centered view of history to a world-centered view in which Asia takes a prominent place instead of being relegated to side comments. He devotes as many letters to Asia as he writes on Europe. Southwest Asian history was included by most European writers mainly because it affected European history. Jawaharlal, while taking Southwest Asia into account, also deals substantially with Chinese, Korean and Japanese civilizations, Indian civilization, and gives some accounts of the Southeast Asia (often left out in other world histories), detailing the rise and glory of Kamboja and Angkor (36), the empires of Sri Vijaya (46), Malayasian empire of Madjapahit and Malacca (78), Farther India in the Southeast Asia, and the treachery of the British and the Dutch against each other for grabbing control of the islands (119), the Philippines and the invisible empire of the United States (121). Though the sub-Sahara African civilization receives less detailed attention, mention is made of Ethiopia and Sudan, East Africa and other regions in a number of survey letters. He gives an account of the admirable civilization of the Maya, Inca, and Aztec empires in pre-Columbian America, and even makes the suggestion from the Chinese source that the "Chinese monk named Hui Sheng journeyed across the eastern seas" and visited the land "called Fu Sang" several thousand miles east of China, probably the land of the Mayas and the Aztecs, in the pre-Columbia America (p. 114). He apologizes for not being able to give some account of Australia, prior to its conversio: into an exclusive outpost for the transplanting of excess population from Europe. Thus, there is a general tendency in these letters to place Europe in its geographic and historical context, and take note of human activity in all the quarters of the globe.

Of special interest among the letters are the surveys of world situations and occasional comparisons and contrasts of the historical events in Asia and Europe. The two continents Jawaharlal sees as the two extensions of the same land mass. In letter 4, "Asia and Europe," Jawaharlal compares the rise and fall of Asia and Europe to the ups and downs of a see-saw in time. "Today Europe is strong and powerful," he states, "and its people consider themselves the most civilized and cultured in the world. They look down upon Asia and other peoples, and come and grab everything they can get from the countries of Asia" (p. 9). But this present-day situation should not be taken as the basis for judging their relative importance or contribution. He asks Indira to look at the map and discover the proportions of the two continents: "See little Europe sticking on the great Asiatic continent. It seems to be just a little extension of it," while Asia is sprawling like a big, lumbering giant. Yet size is not necessarily the test of a man's or a country's greatness. Though Europe is smaller of the two, by historical process it has grown up in recent centuries, emerging from its own underdeveloped days by borrowing or stealing the know-hows from Asia, and developing its own technology. For example, the technology of printing press which produced the revolutionary changes in the fifteenth century, Gutenberg lifted up from China without paying copyright royalties or licence fees as the Europeans charge today for the transference of such technology. Travelers like Marco Polo and others have testified to the manufactures of Asia which were eagerly sought by Europe (letter 69). The currents of civilization, thus, once ran from Asia to Europe long before they were reversed from Europe to Asia, and perhaps that trend will not remain unchanged in due course of time.

From another point of view Jawaharlal gives altogether a different glimpse of the historical movement of people and ideas across the continents. "For long periods and stretches of time," he points out, "Asia has been dominant." Her people went in wave after wave and conquered Europe. Whether they were Indo-Europeans, or Ural-Altaic, Scythians, Huns, Arabs, Mongols, Turks, they all came from somewhere in Asia and spread out in Europe. Indeed, Europe was for a long time "a colony of Asia and many people of modern Europe are descendants from these invaders from Asia" (p. 10). Yet it is Europe that has dominated Asia in the last four centuries. The causes of these changes and the fall of empires and civilizations Jawaharlal suggests are partly internal and partly external:

> Civilizations, like empires, fall, not so much because of the strength of the enemy outside, as through the weakness and decay within. Rome fell not because of the barbarians; they merely knocked down something that was already dead. The heart of Rome had ceased beating when the arms and legs were cut off. We see something of this process in India and China and in the case of Arabs. The collapse of Arabian civilization was sudden, even as their rise had been. In India and China the process is long drawn out and it is not easy to spot it. (p. 180)

In spite of this flow of people, whether by nomadic wanderings, military conquests, colonization, or by religious or commercial crusades, Jawaharlal points out, the two continents have contributed to the cultural stock of mankind in their own creative way. Many countries of Europe have produced "great men of science who have by their discoveries and inventions advanced human civilization tremendously and made life easier for millions of men and women. They have had great writers, thinkers, and artists, musicians, and men of action. It would be foolish not to recognize the greatness of Europe" (p. 10). At the same time, he argues, it would be equally foolish "to forget the greatness of Asia." One should not be carried away by the glitter of modern Europe and forget the earlier glitter of Asia which produced great civilizations, leaders of world thought who have influenced mankind more than anyone or anything else: the founders of principal spiritualities which shaped man's attitudes to life and action, molded social institutions, and humanized group and tribal loyalties into humanistic attitudes recognizing the commonness of mankind. All these men-divine, avatars, prophets, masters, and moral gurus, and the ways of life they established emerged out of the cultural and spiritual foundations from Asia:

Hinduism, the oldest of the great religions existing today is of course the product of India. So also is its great sister-religion Buddhism, which now spreads all over China and Japan, Burma, Tibet and Ceylon. The religion of the Jews and Christianity are also Asiatic religions, as their origin was in Palestine on the west coast of Asia. Zorastrianism, the religion of the Parsis began in Persia, and you know that Mohammed, the prophet of Islam, was born in Mecca in Arabia. Krishna, Buddha, Zoroaster, Christ, Mohammed, Confucius, and Lao-Tzu—the great philosophers of China—you could fill pages with the names of the great thinkers of Asia. You could also fill pages with the names of the great men of action of Asia. And in many other ways I could show you how great and vital was this old continent of ours in the days gone by. (p. 10)

Thus, Jawaharlal contends, by observing the movements in history and march of people and ideas in visionary glimpses, one could come to develop a larger world view and get out of the cave of the mind, for the essence of history is change. "Nothing in the world that is alive remains unchanging. All Nature changes from day to day, minute to minute, only the dead stop growing and are quiescent. Fresh water runs on, and if you stop it, it becomes stagnant. So also with life of a man or the life of a nation" (p. 8). It is important to remember this great noble truth of Buddha, the truth of change. Whether such changes were brought about by invasion, conquest, war, revolution, decay, or death—they are but various forms of transformation in the ever-changing cycles of life and its institutions. This wheel of change and its revolutions only deliver people to another cycle of civilization, and such a change, Jawaharlal wanted his little daughter to know, was taking place in Asia and in India: "How times have changed! But they are changing again even before our eyes. History usually works slowly through the centuries though sometimes there are periods of rush and burst-ups. Today, however, it is moving fast in Asia, and the old continent is waking up after her long slumber. The eyes of the world are upon her, for everyone knows that Asia is going to play a great part in the future" (p. 10).

V *World View*

Glimpses of World History is a remarkable book which challenges ordinary critical judgment. Everything in it is informal and im-promptu, yet one is awed by the breadth of Jawaharlal's culture and the scope of his memory. Being written in prison without the benefit of a reference library, it can also be regarded as one of the great intellectual feats of the century. "I cannot believe," observed Bertrand Russell in reviewing the book, "that any politician in the Western world knows as much history." In spite of the cursory recall of the past in the form of letters, there is coherence and design in the work.

One outstanding impact of the book on the reader is that it emphatically advances the argument for molding "world view of history" on a global pattern. Without this mental adjustment, Jawaharlal seems to argue that the world community could not come together as a world republic. He traces the prevalence of the idea of world state in China whose "universal emperor" ruled as the "son of heaven" and those who were outside his domain were called the "barbarians." Similar ideas of world sovereign or *chakravarti raja* were also current in the Indian tradition, and those who were outside his rule were called the *mlechhas*. Emperor Bharat who has given his name Bharatavarsa, or Bharata to the Indian subcontinent, was a *chakravarti*; so also Yudhishthira, the eldest of the five Pandava brothers in the *Mahabharata*, was crowned with world sovereignty. The same idea of world state also finds expression in the Roman civilization. Though the forms of expression of such ideas have withered away, the ideas themselves have continued to survive and continue to agitate mankind in a search for new forms of the ideal society. "Great empires have risen and fallen," Jawaharlal observes, "and been forgotten by man for thousands of years, till their remains were dug up again by patient explorers from under the sands that covered them. And yet many an idea, many a fancy, has survived and proved stronger and more persistent than the empire" (p. 951).

Because the ancients lacked the knowledge about global geography, the immediate neighborhood of their experience was "the world" which they sought to unite under one rule, and thus establish the world state. So Alexander conquered "the world" and the Romans established themselves as the masters over "the world," without their realizing that there were other nations and continents outside their known world. Little did the Greeks and the Romans know that on the eastern end of Asia the Chinese also called themselves the masters of "the world," and the Indians were also crowning their *chakravartin rajas* as world sovereigns. The one world idea towards which many societies in the past strove with military, religious, or racial, or political might, and for which idea the world struggles today with economic might, Jawaharlal feels, can only end in disintegration and disaster. In his internationalism, his visionary world republic can only remain a dream sensation so long as men are committed to nationalism, regionalism, or other ethnic groupism. Consequently, it is only in dream consciousness that man can realize the potential for a world state at this stage. It is for this reason that Jawaharlal would have the "glimpses" of world history to provide people with the reality of revelation of such a necessity.

Jawaharlal admits that the history he learned in schools and college—mainly Indian history as the British wrote it, and British history—did not help him to come to the global view of history, for the school history that was taught was "largely wrong and distorted" to justify national or imperial purpose (p. 9). Even in the writing of history one needs a vision to perceive the larger sweeps and broader currents, and it is here that Jawaharlal succeeds not because of his facts and paucity of references, but because of his poetic vision and aesthetic sensibility. The *rishis* of the Upanishads and Plato could not communicate their profounder metaphysical visions without the literary form, and it is in the vehicle of literary expression used by Jawaharlal that history achieves visionary form, and Jawaharlal's writings become infused with autobiographical directness and lyrical effervescence.

Jawaharlal's writings disclose some basic attitudes of the writer: his rationalism, his globalism, his humanism, and his moralism. In his view of history which is sweeping waves upon waves as on the face of the ocean, the central hero is man evolving. Men build; men destroy, and surviving men build again on the ruins; but sometimes there are no survivors! Yet the values that a civilization creates are not exclusive or monopolistic. They are universal in character while finding expression in a particular time in history and a particular set of circumstances. The ideal of *dharma*, or the law of righteousness for a good way of life, the ideal of *artha*, the law of well-being and social fulfillment, the ideal of *kama*, the pursuit and fulfillment of love and beauty, and the ideal of *moksha*, the law for the reintegration and rehabilitation of the spirit—all these are fundamental values which have been expressed and reexpressed again and again in different forms. The form fossilizes while the social expression of the ideals decays, and the values themselves survive in the memories and the collective unconscious of the people. Consequently, Jawaharlal seem to suggest that history is one, but the ways of its recording are many.

Finally, in his usual candor, indulging in self-conscious self-analysis, Jawaharlal examines the identity of the "gaol-bird" that soars to survey the global view in which attempt he has left behind a prodigious "mountain of letters":

> I am not a man of letters, and I am not prepared to say that the many years I have spent in gaol have been the sweetest in my life, but I must say that reading and writing have helped me wonderfully to get through them. I am not a literary man, and I am not a historian; what, indeed, am I? I find it difficult to answer that question. I have been a dabbler in many things; I began with science at college, and then took to the law, and after developing various other interests in life, finally adopted the popular and widely practised profession of gaol-going in India! (p. 950)

In spite of himself, this politician-prisoner with a literary style of his own, while recollecting world history for his little daughter, and even helping to make history himself, nevertheless contributed a fascinating classic to Indo-English literature.

CHAPTER 6

Self-Expression: An Autobiography (*1936*)

I *Record of an Epoch*

JAWAHARLAL, the writer and the artist, matured into his finest literary expression in his masterpiece, *An Autobiography* (London, 1936), in which he portrayed himself and an epoch. His kaleidoscopic self-examination by the very nature of his involvement, includes the historic period in India's freedom movement in which he participated and which he spearheaded since 1928. It also focuses on various individuals in the national and world scene of the time, with whom he was associated and came in contact or conflict. This personal record of a politically oriented, idealistically inclined, romantic humanist gives a heightened awareness of the forces that were in conflict in the Indian subcontinent, as viewed by one of its leaders in the middle of that struggle itself, while at the same time identifying that struggle as a part of the larger world conflict in the continuing sweeps of global history.

The *Autobiography* is unique in the circumstances of its recording inasmuch as it was written in the brief spell of eight months during one of Jawaharlal's longest political imprisonments by the British government. In prison he was without the help of reference material except the surprisingly large reservoir of his unusual memory. Yet what he was recollecting and expressing was his own experience in the crowded moments of his life in and outside prison. His reflections, therefore, having the force of postmortem on political events in a continuing struggle, not only illumine some of the subtler political and economic aspects of the struggle but also bring to light the sincerity of the man, his anticipation of consequences of events and actions, his warnings, and above all, the nature of his thinking and the wisdom of the course of action he followed.

Jawaharlal's *Autobiography* coming soon after Gandhi's own unusual record of his struggle in *The Story of My Experiments with
Truth* (in Gujarati in 1925, and in English translation under his own
supervision by Mahadev Desai in 1936), gives another dimension of
the Indian freedom movement. While Gandhi had moral commitment to nonviolence, Jawaharlal only saw in it a policy for a particular goal. Thus the independence movement becomes reflected in
the two autobiographies under two different points of view, one
complementing the other. Besides, both the autobiographies, while
preserving the historical details of the epic struggle in a literary
form, contribute two masterpieces to modern Indian literature by
the uniqueness of their emotional and psychological approach and
appreciable literary qualities.

II   *Seventh Imprisonment*

In his preface Jawaharlal states that the entire *Autobiography* was
written during a brief spell of eight months in prison between June
1934 and February 1935 in his forty-fifth year. In those days, under
Christian Britain, men of goodwill in India were on trial, from the
Mahatma down to the last Satyagrahi, thousands of them. Britain
was doing better than pagan Rome. While Jesus was tried only once
for preaching brotherhood of man and goodwill towards his oppressors, in the land of Buddha who had taught compassion even to the
meanest foe, Gandhi and other Indians were tried and imprisoned
over and over again for the same offence under the usual charge of
sedition. It was a wonder how Britons who butchered their autocratic kings to secure democracy and freedom could not hear the
message of Indian nationalists seeking the same goal of democracy
and freedom, in Jawaharlal's words, from "unchecked despotism"
of imperial Britain.

When Jawaharlal was arrested for the seventh time on February
12, 1934, and sentenced for two years in prison, he was not so much
worried about himself, but was more concerned about Britain losing
its moral soul. For unlike France, the United States, and Russia who
sought freedom through guillotine, sword, and the barrel of the gun,
India was on an experiment to win that freedom through nonviolence. For this experiment to succeed it was necessary to keep Britain
morally alive. It is this concern for the success of the historic experi-

ment under Gandhi on a mass scale that makes the autobiography of Imperial Britain's prisoner devoid of rancor or satire, and endows it with a compassionate understanding. To appreciate the pressure of events and Jawaharlal's psychological response, it would be relevant to examine some of the circumstances leading to the writing of this extraordinary document.

Jawaharlal was out of prison for about five months, during which time he was inevitably drawn into the freedom movement. On January 15, 1934, Jawaharlal took Kamala to Calcutta for treatment. While he was there he witnessed the police brutalities on peaceful demonstrators, and in response, he made three speeches in his usual candor, pointing out the callous manner in which a foreign government suppressed elementary freedoms of people in their own homeland. Thereafter leaving Calcutta, Jawaharlal spent ten days touring the earthquake hit areas of Bihar attending to some of the arrangements of Congress relief work. When he returned to Allahabad on February 11, he was "dead tired."

Next day, late in the afternoon, when Jawaharlal and Kamala "had finished tea and were standing in the veranda" a police car drove up in front of their house and the deputy superintendent of police stepped out. Making it less embarrassing to the official, Jawaharlal did not ask him "Whom are you looking for?" but acted as if he read the thoughts of the empire in that official's face: "I knew immediately," Jawaharlal wrote, "my time had come, I went up to him and said: 'I have been waiting for you for a long time.' He was a little apologetic and said that he was not to blame" (pp. 491–92). The warrant of arrest was from the Imperial British Government through its agent in Calcutta; the Imperial agent in Allahabad was not to be blamed. So after he had been out for five months and thirteen days, Jawaharlal went again back to the seclusion and loneliness of the prison. He did not yell at his imperial tormentors but only became painfully aware of the larger sufferings arising from his internment. "The real burden was not mine," he realized as he thought of the Mary and Mary Magdalene of the situation. "It had to be shouldered, as always, by the women folk—by my ailing mother, my wife and my sister" (p. 492). This tone of subdued compassion marks the general attitude of the autobiography written by a professional "gaol-bird," as he called himself.

In the twentieth century, Britain had improved upon the colonial Romans of two thousand years ago, in publicly washing its hands clean of many sins and calming its uncomfortable Christian conscience. There were Indian magistrates to try, Indian prosecutors to charge, and Indian police inspectors to give witness against Indian freedom fighters, and apparently the sporting English enjoyed this "cricket in the courtroom," in the name of upholding "law and order."

British titled *Rai Bahadur* T. N. Sadhu, the Public Prosecutor of Calcutta, charged Jawaharlal on February 15, 1934: "This gentleman delivered three speeches" in Calcutta on January 17 and 18. "The language used by the accused in his speeches would go to show that he intended to bring the Government into hatred and contempt."[1] The prosecutor's charge was backed by seven Indian police officials of the Criminal Intelligence Department. When the Chief Presidency Magistrate S. K. Sinha was convinced, he framed the charge, and formally read it to the accused. Jawaharlal, as was customary with the Congress Satyagrahis, refused to make any plea or participate in the proceedings. However, he asked to make a statement, if the magistrate permitted it, and the permission was granted to the distinguished prisoner.

Jawaharlal congratulated the reporters "for the very good transcripts" of his statements. He congratulated the government of Bengal for trying him in Calcutta and thus helping him to associate with the suffering of the people of Bengal for the national freedom. Further, he admitted to the court's charge of sedition not merely on the evidence of others but on his own declaration inasmuch as for many years before this his activities had been deliberately seditious, "if by sedition was meant the desire to achieve the independence of India and to put an end to foreign domination."[2] At this point the Indian Public Prosecutor, the British titled *Rai Bahadur* T. N. Sadhu (acting contrary to the nature his name would suggest), got furious, and asked the erring colonial Indian magistrate: "Is the accused entitled to make another seditious speech in the Court?" The apologetic magistrate, afraid of losing his job and incurring the Imperial wrath, cut the statement short, and delivered his comical judgment.

S. K. Sinha's judgment dated February 16, 1934, takes into account all the testimony given in the court, including the unfinished statement of Jawaharlal. "A cursory perusal of the speeches," stated the magistrate, "shows that they are animated by an implacable hostility to the established government." After detailing some of the political disturbances in the country in an effort to decolonize it, he conscientiously continued to state: "For this he [Jawaharlal] attributes the blame not to any individual or group of individuals but to a system, a cruel and vicious system that afflicts all who adopt themselves thereto; it is this machine, he says, that crushes the whole country. He goes on to speak of the innate and inherent vulgarity of Imperialism, its utter cruelty and its vandalism, its shamelessness, its callousness. There is good deal more in the same strain."[3] Perhaps the Indian magistrate, in spite of his colonial office could not help condemning the Government indirectly by animating Jawaharlal's statement in his own judgment. Finally, having soothed his conscience, Sinha found Jawaharlal guilty of the charge of sedition and sentenced him for two years in prison.

Jawaharlal who had studied Law in England was used to the judicial mockery by Britain in India for a long time. So he accepted his seventh sentence like a satyagrahi. "Again the black Maria" of white Britain, he wrote, "carried me back to prison." Through the tiny peephole in the prison van, Jawaharlal noticed the outside world as he passed along. After two and a half months, Jawaharlal was transported from Alipore Gaol in Calcutta to Dehra Dun Gaol where he had been detained earlier. As an old resident of that prison, he was allowed the privilege of having newspapers. And among them, one day, he noticed in the *Manchester Guardian*, "Austrian democracy has been destroyed, although to its everlasting glory, it went down fighting and so created a legend that may rekindle the spirit of European freedom some day in years to come" (p. 499).

Jawaharlal could not help musing over this "moving passage" but he wondered in the British prison "how can it be that the *Manchester Guardian* or the many lovers of freedom who undoubtedly exist in England should be so oblivious to our fate? How can they miss seeing here what they condemn with such fervour elsewhere?" (p. 499).

These various events leading up to his imprisonment and his reaction to them, perhaps give the general attitude of Jawaharlal who was to see himself and others in the context of the great cause to which he was committed. For the autobiography is less of the personal story of the man, or the story of the literary evolution of an aesthete, or of the making of a historian; it traces the making of a man of aristocratic temper and of humane disposition, one who was ready to accept the subordination of his own personality to the cause under the leadership of Gandhi, even when he disagreed with his leader. Because he was neither a moralist nor a doctrinaire, he was able like a practical politician to follow a policy, and as such he later became the Prime Minister of independent India and emerged as a world statesman. It was in this context of an unfulfilled man, in the middle of the undecisive struggle that the autobiography was commenced in June 1934.

III   *Prison Life*

Jawaharlal's prison cell in Dehra Dun Gaol was not a library nor a comfortable living room conducive to luxuriate in remembrances of things past. It was an "old cattle-shed cleaned up and fitted out. The surrounding wall which was ten feet high, had just been raised, especially for my benefit, by another four or five feet. The view of the hills I had so looked forward to was completely cut off and I could just see a few tree tops" (p. 553). Under these circumstances he grew "lonely and cut off from the world" being kept apart by himself. As the physical and the mental sufferings increased, he felt more keenly that "on the other side of the wall, only a few feet away, I knew there was freshness, fragrance, the cool smell of grass and soft earth, and distant vistas. But they were all out of reach and my eyes grew weary and heavy, faced always by those walls" (p. 553).

The outside world also worried him in the prison. While the veteran Congress leaders sincerely committed to complete political and economic independence were undergoing prison sentences, careerists and opportunists got into the Congress. As a result, Congress "seemed to possess two faces: a purely political side was developing like a caucus; and the other aspect was that of a prayer meeting, full of piety and sentimentality" even though "the enigmatical and elusive personality of Gandhi" dominated the scene. While Jawaharlal was still in prison, the Congress Working Committee passed a resolution abandoning the economic revolution, assuring safety and security to feudal landlords and monopolies. This had a "painful effect" on Jawaharlal. On the side of the British Government, "there was an air of triumph, in no way concealed, at what they considered the success of their policy in suppressing civil disobedience and its offshoots" (p. 559).

But apart from Congress politics, more pressing on his mind was Kamala's declining health. She suffered ill-health in the British prison from which she never completely recovered. As she was sinking, Jawaharlal realized that Kamala was again in the grip of her old disease and he felt helpless and unable to be of any service to her. "I knew" he wrote, "my presence by her side would have made a difference." Under these severe physical and mental strains, life was not normal for Jawaharlal in the prison:

My nerves were obviously in a bad way in those days. My sleep became troubled and disturbed, which was very unusual for me; and all manner of nightmares came to me. Sometimes I would shout out in my sleep. Once evidently the shouting had been more vigorous than usual, and I woke up with a start to find two gaol warders standing near my bed, rather worried at my noises. I had dreamed that I was being strangled. (p. 556)

Thus Jawaharlal was torn between his conflicting loyalties and desires, between his political ideal, social goal, his family's future, while his own future was hanging in the air. He felt his elements were dissolving and his life was shattering. In that state to reassure himself he commenced his long lonely pilgrimage backwards, to have glimpses not of the world but of himself as he had lived his life, and how he ended up in the British prison for the seventh time:

Distressed with the present I began thinking of the past, of what had happened politically in India since I began to take some part in public affairs. How far had we been right in what we had done? How far wrong? It struck me that my thinking would be more orderly and helpful if I put it down on paper. This would also help in engaging my mind in a definite task and so diverting it from worry and depression. So in the month of June 1934, I began this 'autobiographical narrative' in Dehra Gaol, and for the last eight months I have continued it when the mood to do so has seized me. (p. 559)

Though the writing of the autobiography was completed in eight months, there were intervals when he felt no desire to write. There were a couple of gaps of about a month. Yet he managed to continue the narrative. One such gap came in August. On August 11, 1934, he was taken from Dehra Dun to Allahabad where he was told he had been "released on parole" temporarily so that he might visit his ailing wife. Jawaharlal had a respite of eleven days outside prison during which time he saw Kamala wax and wane. As he sat beside her for long hours he recollected their eighteen years of married life, consisting mainly of many long absences in separate prisons, and her recurring illness. "Our rare meetings became precious," he noted, "and we looked forward to them and counted the days" (p. 562).

But that was not for long. The police came and rearrested Jawaharlal on August 23, to detain him in Naini prison.

While the ordinary criminal got remission of his sentence for good behavior, a political satyagrahi under British rule was in a worse situation. Eleven days of parole were meticulously added to Jawaharlal's remaining term. About the middle of September he was transferred to Almora Prison. To ease their consciences perhaps, the British officials let him go now and then to see Kamala but it was neither a solace nor any kind of help for he felt more anguished at his being not able to do anything definite or planned to take care of his wife, except now and then go and see her miserable condition. Under this mental torture he continued to write his story and passed his forty-fifth birthday on November 14, in the prison. In January his mother suffered a stroke in Bombay where she was recovering from some treatment. This news added to his mental stress, as he proceeded on his weary journey.

Finally Jawaharlal arrived at chapter 67, "The Epilogue," with a quotation from the Talmud: "We are enjoined to labour; but it is not granted to us to complete our labours." With that awareness he concluded his narrative: "I have reached the end of the story. This egotistical narrative of my adventures through life, such as they are, has been brought up to date, February 14, 1935, District Gaol, Almora" (p. 595). One has to have the humility of a brooding and suffering Hebrew to recognize the egotistical nature of one's autobiography. Yet his mind was echoing with vague questions about his life, about his work, his writing in the prison, the nation's freedom, the world's conflict, and the passing of the seasons:

> The years I have spent in prison! Sitting alone, wrapped in my thoughts, how many seasons I have seen go by, following each other into oblivion! How many moons I have watched wax and wane, and the pageant of the stars moving along inexorably and majestically! How many yesterdays of my youth lie buried here; and sometimes I see the ghosts of these dead yesterdays rise up, bringing poignant memories, and whispering to me: "Was it worth while?" There is no hesitation about the answer. (p. 597)

IV   *Family Crisis*

In May 1935, while Jawaharlal was still in prison, Kamala grew worse and family friends took her to Germany for treatment. Distraught over her fate, Jawaharlal spent another four months in the prison anxiously expecting news about her. Finally on September 4, 1935, he was released on suspended sentence, with the understanding that he would be arrested again to serve the full sentence. Jawaharlal left for Europe and reached Badenweiler, Germany on September 9.

In Badenweiler Jawaharlal read chapters of his autobiography to Kamala and she cheered up to the new situation. On October 25, Jawaharlal wrote a postscript adding a few more details. When Jawaharlal visited London in December 1935 and again in January 1936 he finalized the publication of his autobiography by John Lane, The Bodley Head. He wrote a preface on January 2, 1936. By the end of January Kamala was removed to Lausanne, Switzerland. She was more cheerful and there was marked change in her condition.

While Jawaharlal was in Europe he had been elected in absentia the President of the Indian National Congress which was scheduled to meet in April. Jawaharlal got the news in London in January. He was anxious to return to India, and discussed the matter with Kamala. She was willing and unwilling about Jawaharlal leaving her, yet a passage was booked for February 28. As the time came near Kamala went ahead of Jawaharlal; she died on February 28, while Jawaharlal and Indira remaining by her bedside watched her pass away. A few days later when Jawaharlal was on his way to India with an urn containing Kamala's ashes he felt a continuous ringing sound in his mind which he could not resist. And the sound echoed in the unfathomable emptiness within him: Kamala is no more. As the plane stopped over at Baghdad, he cabled to his publishers in London, dedicating his autobiography: "To Kamala who is no more." In the spring of 1936 the book was published under the title, *Jawaharlal Nehru: An Autobiography, With Musings on Recent Events in India.*

V *Scope of the Survey*

An Autobiography, as published in 1936, contains sixty-eight chapters, a preface, a postscript, and three appendices. In 1940 at the request of his publishers, to make the narrative up to date, Jawaharlal added another chapter, "Five Years Later," which was included in the reprint of 1942. In the United States, the autobiography was published by John Day Co., New York, in 1941 under the title, *Toward Freedom: The Autobiography of Jawaharlal Nehru*. Some brief excerpts from this book were privately printed by that firm in the

same year under another title *Point of View*. A paperback edition of
Toward Freedom was issued by Beacon Press, Boston, in 1958, containing as introduction Jawaharlal's article in the *Modern Review* of
Calcutta (November 1937), entitled "Rastrapathi" under the pseud-
onymn "Chanakya," the famous Indian statesman of the third century B.C. and author of the political treatise, *Artha Sastra*, almost
two thousand years before Machiavelli. Jawaharlal wrote this article
arguing against his own re-election as the President of the Congress,
exposing some traits of the ex-president Jawaharlal Nehru, "a social
democrat who has all the makings of a Caesar." This paperback edition also contains a concluding article, "Parting of Ways," a statement dated August 10, 1940, previously published in *The Unity of
India* (1941), and six appendices. In the concluding article Jawaharlal
charged Britain that having deliberately broken its pledge of freedom
to India, and having broken the unity of the nation, it was going in
a different direction by sponsoring the vicious religious electorates
(unheard of in Britain or in the U.S. in terms of Catholic, Protestant,
Presbyterian, Methodist, etc., electorates), especially in a multi-
religious nation. Thus Britain was parting company with fighters for
freedom in order to retain its imperial gains.

In giving a sketch of his life from his birth till his forty-fifth year,
Jawaharlal was viewing his early days of childhood and youth with
mature eyes. Nevertheless, recollecting as many details from his
memory as possible, he devoted the first four chapters (1–4) to his
first twenty-three years, 1889 to 1912, describing his descent from
Kashmir, his birth and childhood in Allahabad, and his education in
England. Thereafter in the next sixteen chapters (5–20) he discussed
his involvement with the freedom struggle in India as a Congress
worker, including his three imprisonments during the thirteen years,
1913 to 1926.

Jawaharlal went to Europe in March 1926, partly on account of
Kamala's medical treatment, and remained on that continent for one
year and nine months. During this period he came in close contact
with the League of Nations and the International Labor Office in
Geneva; Labor and Socialist leaders of Europe and America; liberals and intellectuals of the time: Romain Rolland, Albert Einstein,
Ernest Troller; Indian patriots in exile in Europe, specially those
seeking haven from the British Secret Service in Germany; nationalist leaders from colonized countries of Asia, Africa, and Latin
America at the Brussels Congress of Oppressed Nationalities in

February 1927, in which he took an active part as Congress delegate; Soviet leaders in Moscow in November 1927. To this period of twenty-one months he devoted three chapters (21–23), two for his crowded European experiences and one for the situation in India.

After his return to India in 1927, Jawaharlal indentified the Indian freedom struggle with the world-wide struggle of the oppressed people against imperialism, colonialism, and the resulting capitalism. Therefore, he made "complete independence"—both political and economic—his goal for India. Because of this attitude, he was regarded as an extremist by the British and their Indian supporters. Also because of his uncompromising stand for complete independence, Jawaharlal dared to disagree publicly with his own father, Motilal, and Gandhi. Motilal, the elder Congressman, was then heading the Moderates who were willing to cooperate with the colonial government and were interested in the promised dominion status for India. Gandhi who had come to dominate the Congress was willing to consider the British promise of reform in the colonial administration in the form of dominion status or something near to it, even though Britain had reneged from its earlier pledge of self-rule given during World War I. Jawaharlal, who was a newcomer to the Congress, considered both these approaches timid and passive and detrimental to India. Consequently, in opposition to the Congress's stand of that time, Jawaharlal carried on his own political campaign with the manifesto of complete independence to the masses of India—workers, peasants, students, and youth—and thrived on their growing support. These eight years of intense activity, 1928 to 1935, Jawaharlal superbly records in personalized impressions in the remaining forty-five chapters (24–48). During this period Jawaharlal emerged not only as the national leader but also the international spokesman. Britain could not tolerate such a colonial extremist who was detrimental to the political and economic interests of the Empire. So they imprisoned him as often as they could under framed charges. In the course of these eight years Jawaharlal was imprisoned four times totaling almost five years in prison. Britain's intense efforts to suppress the nationalist resulted in Jawaharlal's emergence as a writer, transcending the prison walls.

In Jawaharlal's *Autobiography* very few chapters deal with his personal life, if a public person like him has any personal life at all. Apart from the two chapters on his childhood and one on his education in England, there are only occasional references to his family life. His father, Motilal, is dealt with at some length not as his father but as the elder Congressman and Liberal who having become dissatisfied with the British tactics changed his mind in favor of complete independence. His mother hardly receives any notice. His wife comes to prominence only in relation to the Congress activities, and specially when she was critically ill and taken to Europe. There is no sign of his daughter, his only child, growing up except as the addressee of some 200 odd letters written to her from various prisons. We do not see many of these domestic relations of Jawaharlal as much as we see his involvement with the Indian independence movement. What he was writing, therefore, was not of Jawaharlal the man, but Jawaharlal the revolutionary, in whom everything else was subordinated to one overall commitment, the freedom of India. In this sense Jawaharlal's narrative is more like the autobiography of the movement, symbolized in the ideals, goals, sufferings, dreams, and darings of one man, who, among others, helped shape that movement and make history.

Because of Jawaharlal's almost total concern for India's freedom, the bulk of the narrative deals with many aspects of that freedom struggle. Some of the chapters could be read as independent essays on burning questions of the day: Noncooperation (10), Nonviolence and the Doctrine of the Sword (12), Communalism (19), No-Tax Campaign (23), Delhi Pact (29), Dominion Status and Independence (52), The Record of British Rule (54), Democracy East and West (60). No doubt, these topics are discussed from a personal point of view. Yet they are discussed in a rational way to make them stand out as topics interpreted by one of the leaders of the movement, not only telling us about the historical events and the leaders of the movement, but also telling us more about their subtler nuances.

What is of interest in the *Autobiography* are not the historical events themselves during two decades but the manner in which they are observed and commented upon. Through the psychological response of the narrator, the narrative becomes charged with considerable human interest. It expresses Jawaharlal's mental attitude, his ideals, his sufferings, his vision and tragedy, his fears and unshed tears at personal and family crises. Since "All that we are," in Buddha's words, "is the result of our thought," so the consequences of actions follow inevitably, be they good, bad, or indifferent. If one sees freedom as becoming a Knight of the British Empire, he becomes an Imperial Envoy and sits at a round-table conference in

London; but if one sees one's own freedom and the freedom of others as being indivisible—freedom from starvation, exploitation, and from bondage—then one becomes a martyr and a sacrificial lamb; one suffers for the sins of others. It is this suffering undertaken by choice that enlarges the spirit and makes one see the world differently.

Jawaharlal, who had all the training and opportunity for a comfortable and prosperous life as a lawyer under the British Empire, chose to renounce that luxury in order to join the freedom struggle. The greatness of the cause and the seriousness of his commitment elevated him above the rut of ordinary men. In this process of intensified involvement, perhaps he saw glimpses of truth in different aspects of life and historical forces, saw the distant ideal more clearly so that he was able to hold on to that ideal in spite of personal discomfort, economic deprivation, physical hardship, harrassment of all kinds and continual imprisonment. But more than material and physical punishments are the torments of the mind and the anguish of the heart which the freedom fighter suffers at the hands of imperial predators. In giving expression to all these varied personal emotions in his *Autobiography* Jawaharlal endows his "Musings on Recent Events in India" with his extraordinary personality. Consequently, this emotionally charged history, at times becoming lyrical in the description of places, events, relations and conflicts, and panoramic vision, and containing in it a miniature portrait gallery, is a magnificent tribute to Jawaharlal's literary capacity in creating a masterpiece of history during solitary confinement in monotonous space within the brick walls of a dull prison. In this sincere book, written almost in conversational style, one cannot but feel being carried away by the sweep of the emotions, however much one may agree or disagree with the author.

The publication of the *Autobiography* was received with considerable acclaim in India and Britain, though there were some who disagreed with Jawaharlal's point of view, and a few who charged that he was inaccurate. Jawaharlal himself acknowledged that the "reviewers in England and India have treated this book with a generosity and goodwill which have been overwhelming."[4] As for those who criticized him, Jawaharlal felt that it was "an unbecoming procedure" for an author to enter into argument with his critics. Since the author had his say in the book it was natural for the critics to have theirs. The charge of inaccuracy he felt needed clarification since he felt that it was based perhaps on not understanding the nature of autobiography. What is an autobiography? he asked as if to raise the literary principle which would determine the literary genre. Since the autobiography cannot be a mere record of events like a chronicle, it has to have something more of the author. And that something more is what makes the autobiography real:

> It is a record of my own thoughts and moods and how they were affected by external happenings. I endeavoured to make this a truthful record of my own mental development. How far I succeeded in doing so, it is not for me to say. But the important thing is not what happened, but how it struck me and what impression it produced on me. This is the test of the truth or otherwise of the book.[5]

Since Jawaharlal maintained that the "primary test of an autobiography is psychological," it must be true to the man and to his thoughts and feelings. What he had written was not a document on policy or crowd-pleasing manifesto; the opinions and conflicts he expressed were true to his being, even though many disagreed with them. But there were many others who shared the responses to which he had given expression: "For though I wrote as an individual about an individual, to some extent I may claim to have represented the mental conflicts of large numbers of others who worked in our freedom movement." In this context what he wrote had reality to him as it had reality to many others. In a true autobiography, therefore, if the writer is sincere to his thoughts, and expresses them accurately, he has performed his duties to the best of his abilities, and if his opinions conflict with some other opinions, that is no reflection on the book:

> If these are my definite opinions must I not express them for fear of offending some people by my criticism of their views? That would be futile and a puerile policy, unbecoming in a public man. We who dabble in public affairs and seek to change the destinies of millions dare not remain quiet on vital issues. I claim the right of free criticism of public policies and I gladly acknowledge this right in others who may be opposed to my views. Only thus can we have glimpses of the truth, and hammer out a right policy. But of course such criticisms should be without malice or ill-will.[6]

Since it is admittedly difficult for any one person to have a correct point of view of a historical event, Jawaharlal seems to have realized the validity of an autobiography of a public person not in accurately stating the events but rather in truly delineating the inner workings of that public person. In so doing Jawaharlal legislated a principle of literary criticism with respect to autobiography.

VI   *Portrait Gallery*

One of the outstanding features of the *Autobiography* is the manner in which Jawaharlal strings together miniature portraits of individuals in his narrative. These men and women with whom he came in contact, suddenly come to life in his narrative, as if charged with energy, and reveal their distinct characteristics in minimal details. In this process Jawaharlal demonstrates his ability to portray others in addition to giving his responses to these individuals and their actions.

Before he commenced his autobiography, Jawaharlal had some experience in delineating human character in biographical sketches. For example, in *Soviet Russia* (1928), there is a pen-portrait of Lenin (Chapter 7), drawn with considerable understanding of the problems of a revolutionary who had lived through the rule of Imperial Tsars. Having suffered imprisonments under Imperial Britain, Jawaharlal seems to have easily identified with a man who put an end to one of such oppressive rules. In *Recent Essays and Writings* (1934), there is a brief portrait of M. N. Roy whose high intellect Jawaharlal admired but with whose methods he disagreed. Jawaharlal met Roy in Moscow in 1927 when both of them were attending the Tenth Jubilee celebration of the Soviet Revolution. But since then Roy had criticised Jawaharlal rather harshly for wasting opportunities leading to an economic revolution in India. To him Jawaharlal was not radical enough to wage a class war, even though Jawaharlal had spoken about the evils of imperialism, colonialism, and the resulting capitalism. Yet in his portrait of Roy, Jawaharlal sympathized with Roy's revolutionary zeal and showed much concern for his deteriorating health in a British prison. The *Glimpses of World History* (1934) provided many occasions to Jawaharlal for drawing in concise statements outstanding characteristics of men and women who had shaped human destinies in the march of history. But these were people of the distant past or from faraway countries, and one could comfortably pass any judgment on them, even from an unconventional point of view.

In writing his autobiography, on the other hand, Jawaharlal was dealing mainly with individuals in contemporary history. To speak candidly about living men and women and to be truthful about his thoughts and feelings in his narrative is a severe test for any autobiographer. Placed as he was in close association with people in the Indian National Congress and outside, in India and abroad, the problem of characterizing his contemporaries was an acute one. In addition to literary gift, he needed a sharp perception of the conflicting forces in which individuals played their parts, and compassionate understanding of human weaknesses. Combining a broad mind and a stout heart, Jawaharlal drew, in the tradition of the gentle art of criticism, a number of portraits which not only illumine the autobiography but also illustrate some of the traits of its author's personality.

Among the character sketches in the *Autobiography*, those from his early childhood experiences are drawn with tender care. For instance, his father's clerk, Mubarak Ali, who entertained young Jawaharlal, comes out refreshingly vivid in his writing:

> Another of my early confidants was a *munshi* of my father, Munshi Mubarak Ali. He came from a well-to-do family of Badaun. The revolt of 1857 had ruined the family and the English troops had partly exterminated it. This affliction had made him gentle and forbearing with everybody, especially with children, and for me he was a sure haven of refuge whenever I was unhappy or in trouble. With his fine grey beard he seemed to my young eyes very ancient and full of old-time lore, and I used to snuggle up to him and listen, wide-eyed, by the hour to his innumerable stories—old tales from the *Arabian Nights* or other sources, or accounts of happenings in 1857 and 1858. (p. 8)

During his school days in England life was easy for Jawaharlal. He saw some oddities among Harrow boys and later heard some "parlour fire-brands" in Cambridge and London, but none of them agitated him strongly. The English boys seemed to him rather dull. He appeared to have been more impressed by his private tutor, Ferdinand T. Brooks, in Allahabad (1900–05), than his teachers in England, for he did not recall any of them with as much detail as he drew the portrait of Brooks.[7]

Though Jawaharlal had as good an education as England could boast of, that refinement was hardly of any value in the British colony, when such a person caught the European contagion for freedom and democracy; for freedom fighters in the colony, in spite of their

British culture, got beaten, kicked, continually harrassed and impri-soned by perhaps the least cultured of the English soldiers or police officials. Jawaharlal too had his full share of this British colonial counter-culture. He had witnessed the colonial officials suppressing with violence the helpless and nonviolent satyagrahis; he also expe-rienced the English police officer's baton on his back for the crime of carrying the Congress flag in a peaceful demonstration. "I felt stunned," he wrote at this crude awakening to the reality of the Im-perial rule; "and my body quivered all over but, to my surprise and satisfaction, I found that I was still standing" (p. 178). Jawaharlal's British culture could not save him from British beating. But other Congress workers were less fortunate. Many of them had broken limbs, bleeding heads, disabled bodies, and some even died of police brutalities, including a national leader, Lala Lajpat Rai (p. 177).

Yet in his portrait of the British people, Jawaharlal did not con-demn the whole British race for the atrocities committed by its col-onial officials. For he knew that the British people in their own home country behaved differently and among them he had many friends who had shown concern for the freedom struggle in India and else-where. He was also convinced that the people and the government of Britain would not treat political opposition as antisocial or criminal, nor suppress such movement ruthlessly or imprison its leaders without due process of law. He was therefore interested in examining the causes that led the British colonials to acquire such extraordinary atitudes and outrageous behavior once they went out of England. In trying to see some justification for this morla lapse, Jawaharlal also lit up a very delicate psychological fringe of mind of the British legionaries who were trying to make a living in India at a terrible cost to the Indian people, and strangely enough to their own inner being.

Among such British people in India, Jawaharlal portrays a few individuals. There is that infamous General Dyer who ordered the massacre of Jallianwala Baugh in April 1919. While traveling in a train to Delhi, Jawaharlal was shocked to hear that same General Dyer boasting, "how he felt like reducing the rebellious city to a heap of ashes, but he took pity on it and refrained." He ordered only a limited massacre, apparently as a concession to Indian freedom fighters! (p. 43).

Another person was the Superintendent of Lucknow District Gaol where Jawaharlal was imprisoned. He was very annoyed at his

English-educated prisoner because he continually read books in prison, and to his further irritation those books were nonfiction, which according to the Superintendent was dangerous. Pompously he had declared to Jawaharlal that he had "practically finished his general reading at the age of twelve," perhaps in contempt of the Indian who was still doing his general reading at the age of forty! "No doubt," mused Jawaharlal, "that this abstention on his part had been of use to the gallant English colonel in avoiding troublesome thoughts, and perhaps helped him subsequently in rising to the position of Inspector General of Prisons in the United Province" (p. 95).

But more significant than these individual portraits are the group sketches or symbolic portraits of British workers in the Imperial service. In many of these Jawaharlal delineated "the psychology of insecurity" of a foreign ruling class among an unwilling people, and the foreigners' acts of blind fury in a selfish struggle for survival at any cost as colonialists, resulting often in massacres of the innocent.

With the launching of the Non-Cooperation Movement by Gandhi, British official circulars characterized Indian Congress workers in their own country as the enemy who according to the colonial government had taken the initiative to launch the offensive against the peaceful British. There was a British occupation army on alert in the country to put down any national uprising. In spite of this superior military strength and physical security, the officials grew insecure from within and were unnerved by the intriguing "non-cooperation." Was it going to be a guerilla war? Was it going to be a mutiny or a rebellion? Was it going to be a cataclysmic upheaval, the nature of which the officials could not grasp? The vagueness and mystery of Gandhi's movement frightened security-conscious foreign exploiters in India: "The nerves of many a British official began to give way," wrote Jawaharlal. "The strain was great. There was this ever-growing opposition and spirit of defiance which overshadowed official India like a vast monsoon cloud, and yet because of its peaceful methods it offered no handle, no grip, no opportunity for forcible suppression" (p. 70).

One of the reasons for this annoying uncertainty and the resulting internal insecurity, Jawaharlal pointed out, was that the British from their childhood were nurtured in the widespread belief that while Britain was struggling to give "law and order" it was confronted by "treacherous colonial people" who hatched out conspiracies in bazaars and crowded lanes. Because of this ethnocentric self-righteous attitude of the British officials, Jawaharlal maintained, "the English-man can seldom think straight on matters relating to these lands of supposed mystery." He never tries to understand that the peoples of the land may want to be left alone without the foreigners meddling in their affairs, and that they are as ordinary and unmysterious and humane as the Englishmen in England. But the colonial Englishman keeps away from the people and gets his ideas about them "from tales abounding in spies and secret societies, and then allows his imagination to run riot" (p. 71). It was this mental fog of the British colonial government which led it to act cowardly in the face of truth and imprison honest men for demanding freedom. These British officials, in Jawaharlal's portrait, appear like a group, functioning with a tribal consciousness, more to be pitied for the futility of their furor than viewed with retaliatory hatred or sarcasm at their beastly behavior:

> So it was in the Punjab early in April 1919 when a sudden fear overwhelmed the authorities and the English people generally, made them see danger everywhere, a widespread rising, a second mutiny with its frightful massacres, and, in a blind, instinctive attempt at self-preservation at any cost, led them to that frightfulness, of which Jallianwala and the Crawling Lane of Amritsar have become symbols and bywords. (p. 71)

Jawaharlal's main contention in drawing this group picture of British officials in India was that "most Englishmen did not believe in the *bona fides* of nonviolence" when the movement was launched. Instead they tried to create reasons to justify their own fears and insecurity (which was due to a moral deficiency) by asserting that Gandhi's movement was a hoax," a camouflage to cover a vast secret design which would burst out in violent upheaval one day" (p. 70). When truth becomes stranger than fiction, men invent a hundred reasons to justify their delusions.

In another group or symbolic portrait of British officials, Jawaharlal penetrates another of the psychological fogs enveloping the colonial mind. After the Bihar earthquake in January 1934, Jawaharlal toured the area to see the relief work organized by the Congress. He was surprised to find the inactivity of the government. In a public statement Jawaharlal criticized this attitude of the colonial officials of not being responsive enough to the sufferings and needs of the unfortunate victims and survivors. Reacting briskly to Jawaharlal's criticism, the British officials stage-managed a public function to

present a testimonial for the good work the government was supposed to have done. This comic demonstration gave Jawaharlal an
opportunity to muse over the snobbery of the British officials. He
pointed out that the British colonial attitude displayed a hostility "to
criticism of Government in India which is a commonplace in Western countries. It is the military mentality which cannot tolerate any
criticism." Like the feudal kings, Jawaharlal suggested, the British
government in India and all its officials assumed that they can do no
wrong, and to charge them as "incompetent" was almost sacrile-
gious:

> The curious part of it is that a charge of inefficiency and incompetence is
> resented far more than an accusation of harsh government or tyranny. The
> latter might indeed land the person making it in prison, but the Government
> is used to it and does not really mind it. After all, in a way, it might almost be
> considered a compliment to an imperial race. But to be called inefficient and
> wanting in nerve hurts, for this strikes at the root of their self-esteem; it dis-
> turbs the messianic delusions of the English officials in India. They are like the
> Anglican bishop who was prepared to put up meekly with a charge of unchris-
> tian behaviour, but who resented and hit out when some one called him foolish
> and incompetent. (p. 485)

A great majority of the portraits which Jawaharlal had sketched
in his *Autobiography* are of his fellow countrymen, contemporaries
and coworkers, who were related in some way or other to the Indian
independence movement. Many of these individuals have acquired
distinction on their own and are well-known in Indian history. But
strikingly unusual in this national portrait gallery are the sketches
of some Indian patriots in exile in Europe. Though there were many
such exiles in Europe Jawaharlal met only a few during his school
days, and a few more came in contact with him during his second
visit to Europe during 1926–27 when he remained there for twenty-
one months getting experience in international politics. By remembering and writing about them, Jawaharlal has preserved some
haunting portraits in his *Autobiography*.[8] Some of these expatriots
were odd, others were unfortunate victims of persecution, and a
good many of them in Germany were seeking haven from British
Secret Service. Jawaharlal describes a few of them giving their individual life style.

In Montreaux, Switzerland, there was an exile, Raja Mahendra
Pratap, "in strange composite attire," semi-military costume with

high Russian boots, with numerous large pockets "all bulging with papers and photographs." Claiming to be the "servant of mankind," he sent his messages printed on postcards to various delegates attending conferences in Geneva. He looked very much "like a character from a medieval romance, a Don Quixote who had strayed into the twentieth century. But he was absolutely straight and thoroughly earnest." That may be the reason why he was exiled from his own kingdom in India (p. 151). There was Moulvi Obeidulla in Italy who had a scheme for the "United Republics of India" to solve the communal problems (p. 151). In Berlin there were many others—pompous Champakraman Pillai, a thorough nationalist who got along well with the Nazis; pauper Virendranath Chattopadhyaya, very humorous and lighthearted but always hard-up. He was at Oxford when Jawaharlal was at Harrow. In spite of "the passage of many years and long wandering, the pull of the home remained" in him. His clothes were tattered and "often he found it difficult to raise the wherewithal for a meal" (p. 153).

But the most vivid picture Jawaharlal drew was of a recluse in Geneva whom he had met in London during his school days. Shyamji Krishnavarma was living with his ailing wife on the top floor of a house in Geneva in a dusty and dingy place, without any help. Though he had plenty of money he did not believe in spending it, and he often walked instead of taking a tram in order to save a few centimes. Shyamji was suspicious of all newcomers whom he presumed to be either British agents or seekers after his money. Yet as one met him one could see in his bulging pockets ancient copies of his old paper the *Indian Socialist*, one of which he would pull out dramatically and point out with excitement to some article he had written a dozen years ago. Shyamji's habitat and circumstances of living acquire a forbidding reality in Jawaharlal's portrait of him:

His talk was of the old days, of India House at Hampstead, of the various persons that the British Government had sent to spy on him, and how he had spotted them and outwitted them. The walls of his room were covered with shelves full of old books, dust-laden and neglected, looking down sorrowfully on the intruder. Books and papers also littered the floor; they seemed to have remained so for days and weeks, and even months past. Over the whole place there hung an atmosphere of gloom, and air of decay; life seemed to be an unwelcome stranger there, and, as one walked through the dark and silent corridors, one almost expected to come across, round the corner, the shadow of death. With relief one came out of that flat and breathed the air outside. (p. 149).

Jawaharlal admired the sacrifices made by many of these political exiles who "felt they were playing a historic role; that they were involved in a great and epoch-making undertaking." Many of them had exciting adventures, hairbreadth escapes. Though he sympathized with their suffering, he regretted how they had "dropped out of the Indian world and been forgotten by their countrymen whom they sought to serve" (p. 154).

Another striking portrait of his fellow countryman in the *Autobiography* is that of a man who parted company with the Congress and went against the very grain of India's unity and the concept of unity in diversity. It is not easy to understand the ways of thinking of a person whose views on life, purpose and goals become diametrically opposed to one's own. One is apt to condemn such a person. Yet in his portrayal of the character of M. A. Jinnah, a Congressman of mixed Zoroastrian and Muslim origin, Jawaharlal shows hardly any bitterness but regrets the unhappy turn of events. At one time Jinnah had a strong commitment to the unity of the nation and parity of religions, including Hinduism, Christianity, Zoroastrianism, Islam, and Sikhism. But later Jinnah was catapulted into leading a power-hungry group of orthodox Muslims, and with the enthusiasm of a newly converted, he championed a "two-nation theory" to the sorrow and suffering of millions of people in the subcontinent, advocating the incompatability of India's two major religions. Jinnah belonged to the old guard of the Congress when the best of British suits was a qualification for talking politics in the drawing room. The concept of renunciation as Gandhi or Nehru understood was somewhat foreign to his thinking. Yet in his portrait Jawaharlal sees Jinnah as being misled by reactionary-minded Muslim theologians:

A few leaders, however, dropped out of the Congress after Calcutta, and among these a popular and well-known figure was that of Mr. M. A. Jinnah. Sarojini Naidu had called him the "Ambassador of Hindu-Muslim unity," and he had been largely responsible in the past for bringing the Moslem League nearer to the Congress. But the new developments in the Congress—non-cooperation and the new constitution which made it more of a popular and mass organization—were thoroughly disapproved of by him. He disagreed on political grounds, but it was not politics in the main that kept him away. There were still many people in the Congress who were politically even less advanced than he was. But temperamentally he did not fit in at all with the new Congress. He felt completely out of his element in the Khadi-clad crowd demanding speeches in Hindustani. The enthusiasm of the people outside struck him as mob-hysteria. There was as much difference between him and the Indian masses as between Savile Row and Bond Street and the Indian village with its mud-huts. He suggested once privately that only matriculates should be taken into the Congress. I do not know if he was serious in making this remarkable suggestion, but it was in harmony with his general outlook. So he drifted away from the Congress and became a rather solitary figure in Indian politics. Later, unhappily, the old Ambassador of Unity associated himself with the most reactionary elements in Muslim communalism. (pp. 67–68)

Among Jawaharlal's other innumerable sketches in his *Autobiography* the portraits drawn with affection are of those who influenced him strongly in his career—the Indian masses, his father Motilal, and Mahatma Gandhi. Often he had argued with them, disagreed and even got angry; yet his abiding love for them overcame everything in the end and he mellowed into an understanding with them. During his thirty-three years of involvement with Congress with regard to Indian independence from 1913 to 1946, Jawaharlal matured from a dashing young man dreaming of brave deeds with sword in hand in imitation of Garibaldi into a proper satyagrahi, a disciplined voluntary nonviolent disobeyer of chosen civil law which was decreed and enforced by a foreign government to the detriment of the Indian nation. In such a growth and maturity achieved through renunciation, suffering, economic deprivation and nine imprisonments Jawaharlal lived like a tragic hero in a symbolic drama, and vividly saw the factors that shaped his thinking, influenced him to action, and sustained him through his predicaments. In his *Autobiography* Jawaharlal seeks his own adjustment to these triangular pulls.

When young Jawaharlal returned from England after seven years of academic and professional education, he suddenly found himself amidst Indian peasants as a Congress worker. He was not only a stranger to them but was thoroughly unqualified for his job. Yet by the simple art of patiently listening to their problems he became one with them: "I listened to their innumerable tales of sorrow, their crushing and ever-growing burden of rent, illegal exactions, ejectments from land and mud huts, and beatings; surrounded on all sides by vultures who preyed on them—Zamindar's agents, moneylenders, police; toiling all day to find that what they produced was not theirs and their reward was kicks and curses and hungry stomachs" (p. 52). As he traveled from village to village these peasants came streaming out "in miserable rags, men and women, but their faces were full of excitement and their eyes glistened and seemed to

expect strange happenings which would, as if by a miracle, put an
end to their long misery." Looking at these people, their misery and
their overflowing gratitude, Jawaharlal was moved, and as he saw, he
drew a group picture of the masses of India with himself in a dramatic
role in it.

I was filled with shame and sorrow, shame at my own easy-going and comfortable life and our petty politics of the city which ignored this vast multitude
of semi-naked sons and daughters of India, sorrow at the degradation and
overwhelming poverty of India. A new picture of India seemed to rise before
me, naked, starving, crushed, and utterly miserable. And their faith in us, casual visitors from the distant city, embarrassed me and filled me with a new
responsibility that frightened me. (p. 52)

These peasants, workers, and the masses, Jawaharlal acknowledges, took away the shyness from him and taught him to speak in
public, which the Cambridge education had failed to achieve. For he
had paid fines to the College Debating Society for not speaking even
once in the term. By listening to these peasants he learned, and by
learning he spoke, and by speaking he developed a style, the conversational style which he later used successfully on national and
international platforms. It also became the style of his writings.

This sense of participation in the problems of the peasants, workers, and youth and trying to mitigate their burdens, gave Jawaharlal
"the thrill of mass feeling," the power of influencing the mass and
being influenced by them. In that reciprocal interaction Jawaharlal
discovered a different picture of himself. In his self-analysis he gives
an awareness of his own inner being as well as the outward projec-
tions of his ego in the minds of the crowd as he imagined:

I took to the crowd and the crowd took to me, and yet I never lost myself
in it; always I felt apart from it. From my separate mental perch I looked at
it critically, and I never ceased to wonder how I, who was so different in every
way from those thousands who surrounded me, different in habits, in desires,
in mental and spiritual outlook, how I had managed to gain good will and a
measure of confidence from these people. Was it because they took me for
something other than I was? Would they bear with me when they knew me
better? Was I gaining their goodwill under false pretences? I tried to be frank
and straightforward with them; I even spoke harshly to them sometimes and
criticized many of their pet beliefs and customs, but still they put up with me.
And yet I could not get rid of the idea that their affection was meant not for me
as I was, but for some fanciful image of me that they had formed. How long

could that false image endure? And why should it be allowed to endure? And when it fell down and they saw the reality, what then? (pp. 77–78)

Jawaharlal the congressman who became the idol of the masses and the youth was one aspect of his life. But Jawaharlal the newcomer to the Congress politics who dared to oppose his father Motilal, the leader of the Moderates, was another person. As a young boy Jawaharlal had seen his father in the company of British officials, enjoying prestige and honor in the urban society. As an elder Congressman and a leader of the Moderates, Motilal was for cooperation with the British government and for accepting reforms in the administration. But Jawaharlal had become acclimatized to a different reality of India. When Gandhi introduced his novel program of peaceful noncooperation with an evil agency that oppressed the Indian nation and drained its resources for the benefit of England, there was family conflict between father and son. Jawaharlal saw the point, though he was not convinced of Gandhi's fable-like program of noncooperation; but Motilal could not see any point at all. However, Motilal was gradually awakened to the reality of a foreign government in the country and the presence of the occupation army. This subtle transformation and the agonizing reappraisals he had to make are delicately portrayed by Jawaharlal:

I saw very little of father in those days before the Calcutta Special Congress. But whenever I met him, I noticed how he was continually grappling with this problem. Quite apart from the national aspect of the question there was the personal aspect. Non-cooperation meant his withdrawing from his legal practice; it meant a total break with his past life and a new fashioning of it—not an easy matter when one is on the eve of one's sixtieth birthday. It was a break from old political colleagues, from his profession, from the social life to which he had grown accustomed, and a giving up of many an expensive habit which he had grown into. For the financial aspect of the question was not an unimportant one, and it was obvious that he would have to reduce his standard of living if his income from his profession vanished. (pp. 64–65)

Motilal was a man of strong likes and dislikes. He was attracted to Gandhi as a man, but he was not sure of his untried policies. By his own reasoning and sense of self-respect gradually he was brought step by step nearer to Gandhi's proposed action. Then the accummulated anger culminating in the British massacre in the Punjab and its aftermath filled him. A strong supporter of the British rule and law, he felt deeply "the sense of utter wrong doing and injustice, and the bitterness of national humiliation by a foreign government." Yet in his final decision Motilal was still his own self: "He was not to be swept away by a wave of enthusiasm. It was only when his reason, backed by the trained mind of a lawyer had weighed all the pros and cons that he took the final decision and joined Gandhiji in his campaign" (p. 65). This was a different Motilal from the father Jawaharlal had known in his childhood: the man of aristocratic temper and close friend of many English lawyers and administrators. Jawaharlal was afraid of him then; now Jawarharlal had something to give to his father, his experiences with the peasants, and make it easier for the old guard to join the new.

The greatest single influence on Jawaharlal's life and career was, no doubt, Gandhi with whom he closely associated during two decades. At times he had rare glimpses of that enigmatic personality without being able to fathom his mystery. When Gandhi advocated noncooperation there was disbelief in the minds of Congressmen as to whether they should take Gandhi seriously or not. Though Jawaharlal did not fully grasp the new plan of action, he saw the forcefulness of the calm speaker who advocated the nonviolent non-cooperation: "His language had been simple and unadorned, his voice and appearance cool and clear and devoid of all emotion, but behind that outward covering of ice there was the heat of a blazing fire and concentrated passion, and the words he uttered winged their way to the innermost recesses of our minds and hearts and created a strange ferment there." For Gandhi nonviolence was a "dynamic condition of conscious suffering" and its offshoots satyagraha and noncooperation and civil resistance were "nothing but new names of the law of suffering" which the *rishis* had discovered in ancient times. Gandhi also pointed out that though the road was hard and difficult, it was a brave path and sure to "lead to the promised land of free-dom." Though Jawaharlal and many others felt "nonviolent method was not and could not be a religion or an unchallenged creed or a dogma" but could only be a "policy and a method promising certain results," they followed Gandhi: "We pledged our faith and marched ahead" (p. 83).

There were many occasions when Jawaharlal disagreed with Gandhi and even resented some of his activities and priorities. While Jawaharlal was saddled with executive position in the Congress Gandhi had no such official capacity in the executive but everyone knew that he was "the super-president." In his unofficial position

Gandhi carried on many-sided activities. When he launched the self-reliance campaign under the name *Swadeshi* and propagated Khaddar, Jawaharlal was intrigued. "To some extent I resented Gandhiji's pre-occupation with nonpolitical issues, and could never understand the background of his thought" (p. 192). Again when Gandhi undertook a fast unto death in September 1932, protesting against the British government's communal award, Jawaharlal "felt annoyed with him for choosing a side issue for his final sacrifice—just a question of electorate" and not the question of independence itself (p. 370). Gandhi wrote to Jawaharlal asking for his advice and support for the action already taken. They were in two different prisons. Jawaharlal thoroughly disapproved of the whole method of protest, yet after cogitating over the issues of Gandhi's death and the future of the freedom movement and sensing the futility of the fast, he could only dare to say in a telegram: "How can I presume to advise a magician," and assured him of his affection. The fast had no doubt caused tremendous tremors in the hearts of the people: there were upheavals in India and far away in London the British cabinet reversed its decision on the Communal Award. It was only a magician who could without lifting a finger, sitting in a prison, cancel the decree of an imperial government. Sitting in another prison, Jawaharlal, the rationalist, expressed his profound confusion: "For me the fast was an incomprehensible thing and if I had been asked before the decision had been taken, I would certainly have spoken strongly against it. . . . So unhappy as I was, I put up with it" (pp. 372–73). So much were they apart in their personal convictions and spiritual attitudes yet no two persons worked so closely during those two decades as Gandhi and Jawaharlal so that their names have become inseparable in the epic struggle of India's freedom.

As a person who shared Jawaharlal's life intimately for twenty years from her marriage in February 8, 1916 until her death in February 28, 1936, Kamala appears in Jawaharlal's *Autobiography* like "a shadow to the substance" in a most extraordinary portrait, not in words but in their drowning resonance. Jawaharlal hardly mentions her in any manner. Their marriage is recollected in one dry paragraph (p. 37). What about the bride? There were no words to describe her. But soon thereafter Jawaharlal spends a few hundreds of words describing lyrically the "higher valleys and mountains of Kashmir" which he visited with his cousin after the wedding (pp. 37–39). There are only vague references to Kamala, now and then, in the rest of the autobiography more in connection with her taking over the Congress work when both Motilal and Jawaharlal were imprisoned or either one of them was incapacitated. Kamala herself was arrested and imprisoned, and their "orphaned" child, Indira, kept a dutiful fortnightly vigil at two separate prisons whenever she was away from school.

Kamala was taken to Europe for treatment in 1926 and she remained there with Jawaharlal for one year and nine months as an invisible presence. She was taken again to Europe in May 1935 for treatment but she never recovered. In his postscript written in Badenweiler, Germany, Jawaharlal had only two solitary sentences to write about Kamala. In the preface written in Badenweiler, in January 1936, there is no mention of Kamala at all.

Kamala died on February 28, 1936, and Jawaharlal left for India with her ashes. While on his way flying in a KLM aeroplane from Cairo over the desert, Jawaharlal suddenly became aware of a vast desert within his being, and his terrible loneliness in which he heard a continuous ringing sound growing larger and larger in its echoes: Kamala is no more! He could not resist this drumming within his soul until he got out at Baghdad and cabled to London the dedication of his autobiography "To Kamala who is no more." Like Cordelia's ringing words bursting the silence of reawakened King Lear, "I am, I am," Jawaharlal's dedicating words dissolve into silence, sending ripples of echoes in which Kamala's portrait comes to life, somewhat in Lao Tzu's sense. It was only ten years after her death that Jawaharlal could write a pitiful chapter on Kamala in his *Discovery of India* (1946) recollecting some of the rarest moments they had together in their twenty years of married life.[9]

In concluding his autobiographical narrative, Jawaharlal declared in the epilogue, "More and more I have looked upon life as an adventure of absorbing interest" (p. 596). It was because of this sense of adventure he declined "to seek harbourage" in established ways of life, but preferred "the open sea with all its storms and tempest" (p. 377). As he sailed over the rough seas and lived in and out of prisons, Jawaharlal not only found his real purpose and meaning of life but also painted his own portrait as a man living his adventurous life and writing his "egotistical narrative":

All these shouting crowds, and dull and wearying public functions, and interminable arguments, and the dust and tumble of politics touched me on the surface only, though sometimes the touch was sharp and pointed. My real conflict lay within me, a conflict of ideas, desires, and loyalties, of subconscious depths struggling with outer circumstances, of an inner hunger unsatisfied. I became a battle ground, where various forces struggled for mastery. I sought an escape from this; I tried to find harmony and equilibrium, and in this attempt I rushed into action. That gave me some peace, outer conflict relieved the strain of the inner struggle.

Why am I writing all this sitting here in prison? The quest is still the same, in prison or outside, and I write down my past feelings and experiences in the hope that this may bring me some peace and psychic satisfaction. (pp. 207–8)

CHAPTER 7

Occasional Writings

D URING his brief spells of freedom and intense political life, in between prison sentences, from 1933 to 1941, Jawaharlal wrote, spoke, or issued statements on questions immediately at hand. These occasional writings were collected periodically and published under various titles in India and England. Significant among them are *Recent Essays and Writings* (Allahabad, 1934); *India and the World* (London, 1936), edited by H. G. Alexander; *Eighteen Months in India* (Allahabad, 1938); and *The Unity of India* (London, 1941), edited by V. K. Krishna Menon.

By their very nature, the occasional writings are short and topical. A number of them are but brief press statements of only a few hundred words; others are essays and articles ranging from ten to thirty pages. There are also speeches and messages delivered on different occasions. All of them were occasioned by the immediate necessity of responding to a situation, or making a point clear, or refuting a charge, or at times giving free rein to his imagination in a humorous mood or a discursive travel account. Though the subject matters of these writings vary, what holds them together as if in a cluster, is the central character, Jawaharlal Nehru, who comes alive radiating through his various moods.

The occasional writings demonstrate in unmistakable clarity Jawaharlal's continuing theme of "Complete Independence" from Britain in order to restructure the Indian nation politically, economically, and culturally. They also reveal his uncompromising point of view that freedom is not merely political; to make it meaningful to the people there should be equal economic freedom. Consequently, to whatever subject Jawaharlal addressed himself in prison or outside—whether it was the question of Indian prisoners in the Andaman Islands or the Quetta earthquake, the slave labor in the tea estates or Satyagraha in the cities, he used language with assured skill and confidence. But more than merely using language, his manner of writing endows his works with a sense of history and human interest, and at times sparks of wit and delightful humor.

I Recent Essays and Writings

Recent Essays and Writings contains twenty-one short pieces, including seven short press statements issued on various dates; two articles published in England, five pamphlets on political situation and prison conditions, three messages, two speeches, a pen portrait, and a humorous essay. Most of them were written during the five months Jawaharlal was out of jail from August 30, 1933 to February 12, 1934. The publisher's note declares that because of constant inquiries for Jawaharlal's opinions on the major events of the day, they collected in a single volume some of his important writings and statements "which appear to have more than passing value."

Jawaharlal's opinions are often straightforward and frank. In a press statement, "The Andaman Prisoners," speaking from his personal experience, Jawaharlal deplored the "punitive, vindictive, and barbarous" mistreatment of the prisoners (p. 109). In another pamphlet "Prison Land," he exposed the corruption and brutality existing in the British prisons he had been to in the past years, and urged reforms in the criminal procedures and prison administration. He felt "justice is not entirely blind in India; it keeps one eye open," especially to relieve the colonial functionaries from the clutches of the law (p. 100). In "Fascism and Communism," Jawaharlal expressed his shock at some of the press accusations that he was a Fascist. Refuting the charge, he assented "fundamentally the choice before the world today is one between some form of Communism and some form of Fascism, and I am all for the former, that is, Communism. I dislike Fascism intensely" (p. 126). In two other statements, "Labour and Congress," and "Trade Union Congress," Jawaharlal advocated that the labor organizations should promote progressive programs and seek their fulfillment, even going ahead of the National Congress; but they should also work in cooperation with it toward complete freedom (p. 131). In "Indian States," he declared that the archaic Indian Princely States system "as it exists today must go, root and branch" to facilitate the transformation of feudal principalities into a modern democratic state (p. 133).

Jawaharlal's view of the ideal society was expressed in two short

statements, "Civic Ideal," and "Civics and Politics." He states that
the civic ideal aims at common possession and enjoyment of municipal amenities which continue to increase until they comprise
almost everything that citizens require. When this ideal becomes
national or international then it becomes merged with the scientific
ordering of the world's affairs for the benefit of all people and not a
small group. In other words, utopian society is brought about by the
expanding universe of civic ideal. To him "Communism was the
extension and the application of the civic ideal to the larger group of
the nation and ultimately the world" (p. 136). There is no doctrinaire
approach or theoretical dogmatism to European communism. For
he believed that man being the hero of history, in relation to the
whole mankind as one tribe, there is no place for fragmented groups
like "haves" and "have-nots," "exploiter" and the "exploited,"
"imperial" and "colonial".

Jawaharlal sharply reacted to the question of communalism and
religious antagonism deliberately injected into the freedom struggle
by the British government at the London Round Table Conference
which ended in failure, without solving the fundamental issue of
freedom. Jawaharlal clearly saw that those who indulged actively in
generating communal hatred and spreading communal fear and sus-
picion, represented "the rich upperclass groups, and the struggle for
communal advantages is really an attempt of these groups to take as
big a share of power and privilege for themselves as possible." But
their communal demand did not in any way meet the needs of the
masses nor did they have "any program for the peasants, industrial
workers, the lower middle classes which form the bulk of the nation"
(p. 57). In a "Reply to Sir Mohammad Iqbal" (Sir Mohammad advocated national segregation of the Muslims and cooperation with
the British government) Jawaharlal rejected the idea that the constitution of India should be drafted in London. Instead he offered
the "democratic and feasible solution" of electing a Constituent
Assembly on the basis of adult franchise, in which neither Sir Mohammad nor the British government was interested at that time.

Examining the political situation of the time, Jawaharlal wrote the
pamphlet "Whither India?" and two articles, which were published
in England, "The Indian Struggle for Freedom" (*Daily Herald*) and
"A Letter to England" (*Manchester Guardian*). Since nationalism
was essentially a middle-class phenomenon, the British government,
seeking the support for the Empire, encouraged the feudal, and

capitalistic elements in the Indian society; Jawaharlal wanted to clarify "whose freedom are we particularly striving for." Obviously there was the "feudal India of the princes, the India of big zamindars, of small zamindars, of the professional classes, of the agriculturists, of the industrialists, of the bankers, of the lower middle class, of the workers. There are the interests of foreign capital and those of home capital, of foreign services and home services . . . It is obvious that there are serious conflicts between various interests in the country" (p. 4). To resolve this conflict, Jawaharlal felt that Indians should first recognize that they are a nation and understand that the freedom struggle is "a part of this great world problem and must be affected by world events" (p. 2). For he argued that the course of history showed "a succession of different forms of government and changing economic forms of production and organization. The two fit in and shape and influence each other. When the economic changes go ahead too fast and the forms of government remain more or less static, a hiatus occurs, which is usually bridged over by a sudden change called revolution" (p. 7). Consequently, freedom struggle, Jawaharlal viewed "essentially as economic struggle, with hunger and want as its driving force" (p. 19); but the British were trying hard to demonstrate that it was a religious conflict between Muslims and Hindus, thus making the communal question the primary issue and sidetracking the fundamental demand. What troubled Jawaharlal was not the clever way in which the British combined "their moral instincts with their self-interest" but how the Indian Anglophiles have taken "this unctuous and hypocritical attitude."

In answering his own question, "Whither India?" Jawaharlal stated optimistically that India was progressing towards independence and economic freedom within the framework of an international socialist world federation. "We may not have it within our grasp," he wrote, "but those with vision can see it emerging on the horizon. And even if there be delay in the realization of our goal, what does it matter if our steps march in the right direction and our eyes look steadily in front" (p. 24). He was only surprised how the British and their Indian supporters could be so blind as not to see this march of events.

Jawaharlal's pamphlet was attacked with wildest of furies, charging that he was a leftist prophet blindly leading India to "the Soviet Hell," a man with "poor knowledge of history," who has made jail-going his profession. In a supplementary pamphlet, "Some Criticisms

Considered" and "Further Criticisms" Jawaharlal asserted his un-qualified hope: "I do believe that natural laws will speedily put an end to the British empire and imperialism and capitalism, and I wish to help in the process" (p. 37).

In his two articles originally published in England, Jawaharlal argued that the government of the people, for the people, and by the people of India could only be achieved by decolonization, by un-doing the exploitation and "de-vesting of the great vested interests in India" (p. 117). The gimmick of "Indianization" by which a few handpicked Indians were given jobs in the British colonial adminis-tration would not solve any of the problems.

The real literary contributions in the volume are a pen portrait of M. N. Roy, and a delightful personal essay, "A Window in Prison."

Jawaharlal met Roy, the outstanding Indian radical intellectual, in Moscow in November 1927. He admired Roy's personality and towering intellect, but he did not agree with Roy's commitment to class struggle completely. Roy considered Jawaharlal a playboy brought up in the bourgeois tradition, who because of his upbring-ing would be unable to wrestle with the shrewd British colonists and deliver freedom to the Indian people. In spite of these differences in their attitudes, Jawaharlal's portrait of Roy was not marred by ill-feelings: "I am impressed by him [Roy]. Evidently, he was not im-pressed by me, and during the years that followed he wrote many an article in bitter criticism of me and my kind, whom he dubbed, with considerable truth, as petty bourgeois. He used hard words which stung, but the memory of our brief meeting remained fresh in my mind and I retained a partiality and a soft corner in my heart for him" (p. 110). Roy returned to India in 1931 to take up the cause of Indian revolution, but the democratic British government quickly arrested and imprisoned him. At the time of writing, Roy was se-riously ill and had been for two years in the same prison as Jawaharlal. But the British Government did not let Roy out. Jawaharlal felt that this deliberate waste of human intellect was a national tragedy in colonial India.

In a personal essay, "A Window in Prison," Jawaharlal rambles on his prison experiences in a delightful mock-heroic tone. A po-litical prisoner who is not a criminal, is enclosed within "high walls" because his thinking and acting are considered dangerous for the British colonists. He is effectively cut off from the outside world. But sometimes even such a prisoner finds a chink in the prison wall through which he can peep out. This peephole, Jawaharlal describes, is the newspaper that is allowed to be slipped in, after careful censorship. Through these "windows," narrow and colored by the press controlled by the British, the prisoners are given a restricted and distorted vision. When Jawaharlal viewed the outside world through the window of *The Statesman* he found "The world struggling in the octopus-grip of depression and conflict and doubt and uncertainty; but in this sorry world there was one bright spot, land of India, sheltered from all ills by the British Government" (p. 80). The British editor had found that all troublemakers were either eliminated, exiled, or imprisoned, and thus effectively silenced.

Another source of "delightful romance" for the nationalists in prison was the "Simla Correspondent" of the paper and his fantastic stories. In measured language, he surveyed the Indian political scene, the inner workings of the Congress, and Gandhi's mind; "A few wild men of the Congress were dragging Mr. Gandhi along, although all he wanted was peace and quiet and an opportunity to do solid constructive work." And then, almost as if to spite the correspondent, "Mr. Gandhi changed places with the wild men and became as wild and aggressive as ever, dragging the peaceful Congress along with him. This was obviously not a sporting thing to do; it was not cricket" (p. 84).

II   India and the World

When Jawaharlal was in Europe attending to Kamala during September of 1935 and February 1936, there was a growing interest in England in Jawaharlal's thoughts and ideas. His *Glimpses of World History*, though not published in England was making news. His essays and articles in India and in Europe were taken seriously. When he visited London, some British friends felt that "some of Mr. Nehru's writings on politics, especially some of the most recent, should be available for western readers in a handy and permanent form." In response to this suggestion, Jawaharlal left some of his published and unpublished works with a friend, H. G. Alexander, who selected and edited the material for the book, *India and the World*, (London, 1936).

The editor included fourteen pieces of writings for the volume—two speeches, eleven essays, and one transcript of a meeting held in London in February 1936, which was titled, "Indian Problems." Of the eleven essays, five had already been published in India and four in Europe, and the remaining two were unpublished originals. The justification for the particular selections in the book was that "Mr. Nehru is one of those Indians who continually sees his own country not as an end in itself, but as a part of the world influenced by world forces" (p. 7). The editor wanted the silent majority of the British public to know and understand the way "the domestic issues are again and again related to world tendencies" (p. 8). A few other essays were selected to illustrate the various moods and concerns of one of the most important prisoners of Britain who put his jailers to shame, and secondly, to give the British citizens an opportunity to see themselves through Indian eyes.

Jawaharlal's two speeches were the important Presidential Addresses delivered by him on two critical occasions, developing his thesis of complete independence. The first was given at the Lahore session in December 1929, when he was the newly elected president of the Indian National Congress, ten years after the Jallianwala Bagh massacre. The second was delivered in April 1936, at the Lucknow session when he was reelected the President, after the failure of three London Round Table Conferences during 1931–33 in furtherance of the British promise of some form of self-rule. The Congress had finally come to recognize Jawaharlal's clear-cut demand made in 1922, for complete independence. Britain had ignored this demand for almost fifteen years, dodging the Congress with vague promises about dominion status and provincial autonomy. Jawaharlal's drum call was becoming more and more loud and the editor felt that Britain could not afford to ignore it much longer.

Jawaharlal's election as President of the Indian National Congress in 1928 and 1936 came after he had two critical experiences in Europe: first his participation in the Brussels Congress of the Oppressed Nationalities in February 1927, and his contacts with the liberal thinkers and labor leaders of Europe. On the second occasion, though he was ostensibly attending to Kamala's illness, nevertheless, as the unofficial spokesman of the Congress, he again took up the threads of international politics with which he had become familiar a decade earlier. With these European experiences Jawaharlal was presenting a unique point of view, namely, the way in which Asian freedom movements appeared in Europe in the background of progressive ideals of social justice and labor movements. On both occasions he ridiculed the Congress members for their failure to see that there was nothing to negotiate on the basis of reforms with the colonial administration, since none of the British political parties were willing to concede the idea of Indian independence. He wanted the Congress to realize that the Indian demand for independence was a part of the larger world-wide struggle of oppressed peoples.

Jawaharlal argued that "there is intimate connection between events"; the freedom movement was not causing "disorder" as the colonial powers were trying to make out; on the contrary the freedom struggle was the Karmic consequence of the previous actions by the colonists when they caused disorder by depriving the people of the freedom in the first instance. The freedom struggle was only a natural movement towards the restoration of that equilibrium lost at the time when the predatory colonists created violent disorders in order to establish their domain. The wave of change that was sweeping the world was the spirit of defiance of the oppressed world. Jawaharlal concluded: "Who will take away from us that deathless hope which has survived the scaffold and immeasurable suffering and sorrow; who will dare to crush the spirit of India which has found rebirth again and again after so many crucifixions?" (p. 109). No wonder the editor wanted the British public who supported the British government to read these writings, and realize on which side of the cross they were!

Among the selections included to illustrate Jawaharlal's moods and views were "Whither India?" and "Prison Lands," both of which were published in the *Recent Essays and Writing*; Jawaharlal's first and last letter to Indira in the *Glimpses of World History* (letters 1 and 196); and "The Mind of a Judge."

"The Mind of a Judge" written in prison just prior to his release on September 4, 1935, was published in the *Modern Review*, Calcutta. In this personal essay Jawaharlal rambles amiably about the profession of a lawyer for which he was trained, and how his life style would have been had he remained in his vocation. "I suppose I would have done tolerably well at the bar, and I would have had a much more peaceful, duller, and physically more comfortable existence than I have had so far. Perhaps I might even have developed into a highly respectable and solemn looking judge with wig and gown" (p. 130). Jawaharlal wondered how the mind of such a judge would work when he had to sentence ruthlessly his fellow countrymen for non-political as well as political crimes most of which were patriotic deeds worthy of praise but were offenses only against a foreign government and its economic interest. Whether laws imposed by colonial ordinances and decrees by an autocratic executive had any validity in the absence of the sanction of the people, and whether there could be any "justice" when the judicature itself was based on injustice were larger questions in which Jawaharlal, but no judge under the colonial system, was deeply interested.

As a partial remedy to the caricature of justice under a colonial system, Jawaharlal suggested a mental therapy: "A term of voluntary imprisonment will do a world of good to the bodies and souls of our judges, magistrates, and prison officials; it will also give them a greater insight into the prison life" (pp. 137–38). In support of this proposal, he quoted the notable example of a prison official, Thomas Mott Osborne of famous Sing Sing prison in New York, who trained himself by undergoing a term of voluntary imprisonment, and as a result of this, introduced many "remarkable improvements" (p. 137).

Jawaharlal considered the death penalty far preferable to life imprisonment, for he had come "to realize that there are many things far worse than death" (p. 139). Yet he had delicacy in determining his choice of death: "I would not like to be hung; I would prefer being shot at or guillotined, or even electrocuted; most of all other methods I would like to be given, as Socrates was of old, the cup of poison which would send me to sleep from which there was no awakening. This last method seems to me to be far the most civilized and humane" (p. 139). But unfortunately in India the British Government performed public hanging which reminded Jawaharlal of the methods of the Spanish inquisition.

Finally Jawaharlal came to the realization in prison that "the basic nature of the State is force, the compulsion, the violence of the governing group" (p. 143). It is this violence of the governing group which produces the counter-violence of other groups which seek to oust the government. Yet Jawaharlal wondered curiously, "how the governing group in a State, basing itself on an extremity of violence, objects on moral and ethical grounds to the force of violence" of the revolutionaries. But these were questions beyond the power of ordinary judges, let alone judges under a colonial system, with whose lot Jawaharlal sympathized while suffering the inquity at their hands.

In an article published in *Vendredi* (Paris, 1936), entitled "India and the World" (which lends its name to the volume), Jawaharlal asserted that "whatever big will happen in India will affect the larger world to a great extent." India had affected British foreign, domestic, military, and economic policy for over a century: "The wealth and exploitation of India gave England the needed capital to develop her great industries in the early days of the industrial revolution and then provided her with markets for her manufactured goods" (p. 201). Yet England, while proudly "laying stress on its democratic constitution at home, acts after the Fascist fashion in India" (p.200). When the Indian freedom movement would finally overthrow the empire, Jawaharlal felt a "free India would inevitably play a growing part in international affairs, and that part is likely to be on the side of the world peace and against imperialism and its offshoots" (p. 203–4). When would that freedom come to India? Though Jawaharlal was not sure of the time, he was sure of the goal.

Yet in another article "A Visit to England", published in *The Socialist* (London, 1935), Jawaharlal concluded his impressions of his visit to England rather optimistically: "Whatever the future may hold, I shall carry back with me to India the knowledge that there is a fund of goodwill in England for the Indian struggle, and we have many true comrades here who stand for the same socialist ideal as many of us do and we can work together for a common cause" (p. 217).

In these articles, Jawaharlal was attempting to show how Europe looked from the Asian point of view. There is directness and sincerity in all that he wrote, even when he disagreed. That boldness in opposing the economic interests of the European powers in Asia was motivated not so much by a sense of revenge but a desire to see a new social order in the world.

III   Eighteen Months in India

Eighteen Months in India contains fourty-four selections written after Jawaharlal's return from Europe and assumption of the Congress presidency in March 1936 until it was time to nominate another in August 1937. During this period of eighteen months, Jawaharlal states, he had "functioned on the public stage" when new ideas had spread and new conflicts and difficulties had arisen. Though he was aware that he was not writing the history of that period in those "scrappy collection of essays of varying merit and importance," he was nevertheless conscious that the historical truth was as illusive as any other aspect of the truth which men attempt to comprehend and communicate. Yet he felt that there would be the possibility of reaching some understanding of the historical phenomena in glimpses of intuitive perception; towards that end, he hoped to preserve his "personal reactions to happenings and tendencies" and help somewhat in understanding India of the day and her manifold problems (p. vi).

Scattered among the collection are three personal essays; three critical essays in which Jawaharlal responds to criticism of his writings and speeches; twelve statements on international affairs, nine on India's close relations and problems with her immediate neighbors, and three dealing with Southwest Asians in European situations. The remaining twenty-six selections relate to the work of the Congress and the freedom movement, including two presidential addresses. In these writings Jawaharlal displays two outstanding aspects—first, his growing sense of international relations, and second, his acute sense as a literary critic.

On the international scene, Jawaharlal recognized two sides for contemporary conflicts, irrespective of country, race, or religion, or ideology, namely, the brotherhood of sufferers and demonic enclave of a smaller group of oppressors. In a message sent to the demonstration organized by the Spanish–Indian Committee at the Kingsley Hall in London on April 9, 1937, Jawaharlal observed, "Spain and the Tragedy enacted there, dominate our thoughts today whether we live nearby in the other countries of Europe or in far India. For this tragedy and conflict are not of Spain only but of the whole world" (p. 128). For Jawaharlal felt that the nature of the world conflict was the same: in India it was between the occupying forces of imperial Britain and the Indian people seeking self-rule; in Spain it was between the Fascist forces of Europe and their mercenaries financed by British bankers, and the people of Spain seeking democracy. England, while professing democracy and freedom at home, was abetting and actively supporting fascists for the sake of her own imperial vested interest, indicating thereby that imperial England is as much "a blood-brother" of Fascist Italy as of Nazi Germany (p. 129). Whether it was the massacre in Addis Ababa by Fascist Italy or the massacre in Jallianwala Bagh by imperial Britain, the international position of the two massacres was the same. In their arrogance the Fascists and the imperialists, Jawaharlal pointed out, ruthlessly destroy the people of another nation, and rob them of their resources, indulging in a kind of international banditry or piracy.

Yet many people were bewildered by the seeming inconsistencies and contradictions in the British foreign policy, "in the shameful betrayal in Abyssinia, in the intrigues of central Europe, and in the farce of non-intervention in Spain" (p. 120). But Jawaharlal saw no real inconsistencies, for Britain behaved like an imperial "blood-brother" of Fascist powers. The inconsistency, he pointed, is in the minds of those who imagine that the democratic background of British domestic policy governs the nondemocratic and Fascist foreign policy of the imperial country. Consequently, in the field of international action, Jawaharlal concluded, imperial foreign policy "has pursued consistently and unhesitatingly the path of rapprochement with Fascism" (p. 130); for there can be no such thing as colonial democracy or a vegetarian tiger.

In the light of this common suffering of the people of India under imperialism and the people of Ethiopa and Czechoslovakia under Fascism, Jawaharlal sent his message of sympathy to the people of Spain: "We are ourselves helpless in India, and hunger and stark poverty meet us everywhere; we fight for our freedom and to rid ourselves of the empire that exploits and crushes us . . . But out of our hunger and poverty we will send what help we can to our comrades in Spain, and though this may not be much, it will carry with it the earnest and anxious good wishes of the people of India. For those who suffer themselves feel most for their brothers in misfortune elsewhere" (p. 132).

Reiterating the same attitude towards the suffering of the Semitic people at the hands of Fascist and Imperial powers, Jawaharlal issued two other statements, "The Arabs and Jews in Palestine," and "Spain and Palestine." Stemming from the same stock, Arabs and Jews, Jawaharlal argued, had coexisted in Asia and Africa, in spite of their tribal fortunes going up and down. But those Jews who migrated to Europe had been for centuries subjected to the most terrible oppression in Christian countries. Jawaharlal expressed his deeply felt understanding of the predicament of European Jews, with many of whose leaders he had worked in close relation during the Brussels Congress in 1927:

Few people, I imagine, can withhold their deep sympathy from the Jews for the long centuries of the most terrible oppression to which they have been subjected all over Europe. Fewer still can repress their indignation at the barbarities and racial suppression of the Jews which the Nazis have indulged in during the last few years, and which continues today. Even outside Germany Jew-baiting has become a favorite pastime of various Fascist groups. This revival in an intense form of racial intolerance and race war is utterly repugnant to me and I have been deeply distressed at the sufferings of vast numbers of people of the Jewish race. Many of these unfortunate exiles, with no country or home to call their own, are known to me, and some I consider it an honour to call my friends. (p. 133)

By the very nature of the international conflicts, from Jawaharlal's point of view, the identity of attitudes of Fascist and imperial powers (in generating bitter conflicts by stimulating religious antagonism) becomes manifest, in the hatred and opposition of Christians and Jews in Germany, Catholics and Protestants in Ireland, Jews and Muslims in Palestine, and Hindus and Muslims in India. Yet at times it becomes absurd, in sending sympathies to people suffering in India, Abyssinia, Czechoslovakia, Spain, Germany or Palestine, while at the same time cooperating with that very imperial power and helping it to carry on its oppression and assistance to Fascists to commit aggression, against people struggling for freedom.

Another aspect of Jawaharlal's internationalism was his attempt to establish closer relations with other Asian countries, and to project attitudes independent of British views and propaganda sustaining their own economic and military interests. He strongly protested the use of Indian colonial troops by Britain to carry on its aggressive wars into China, which he maintained was an outrageous affront to two great nations of Asia and to their long traditions (p. 290). Because of British colonial intrigues "the world is drifting helplessly to a state of continuous conflict," for wars begun without declaration do not end easily but bring about death and destruction of thousands of civilians (p. 291). Jawaharlal condemned the use of Indian men and resources to subsidize British international war games, and warned that Congress would use all its strength to paralyze the British in India.

Jawaharlal also visited the neighboring countries of Ceylon, Burma and Malaya which were essentially facing "the same problems and the same opponents" as India, namely, the British imperialism, local feudalism, and international capitalism. The British monopolies were exploiting the natural resources of these countries to the utter detriment of the people of the land. Jawaharlal assured the national leaders in those countries of India's cooperation and solidarity in their common struggle, and wished to reestablish the "cultural and commercial bonds that have tied them for thousands of years" (p. 169). If countries of Europe could work together for a cultural community, he asked, why should the European colonists thwart the growth of such cultural community in Southern Asia?

It was for the first time that the Indian National Congress under Jawaharlal's leadership asserted an independent foreign policy, in opposition to the British colonial apparatus. In fact as the President of the Congress, Jawaharlal was partly fulfilling his own demand made in 1928 for India's need of independent international contacts.

Jawaharlal's major concern during this period was with the freedom struggle. The British government had already introduced a treacherous "wooden horse" in the guise of provincial autonomy and religious electorate, thus providing for "Indian participation" in the colonial government. Jawaharlal warned that for an imperial country, democracy abroad means basically "its own domination and protection of its monopoly interests" (p. 77). He asked whether Britain would allow social and economic changes to take place in the colony if they affected British monopolies. He was convinced that the British government would not hesitate to use any method to hold on to their colonial possesions. In his vision of the contemporary situation, he saw that "democracy and fascism, nationalism and imperialism, socialism and capitalism combat each other in the world of ideas, and as this conflict develops on the material plane, bayonets and bombs take the place of votes in the struggle for power" (p. 79).

Even though Jawaharlal rejected the illusive colonial democracy outright in favor of complete independence, the Congress once again succumbing to the bait, compromised its 1927 goal, and decided to participate in the election limited to ten percent of the population. When the Congress won the election and formed provincial ministries, Jawaharlal refused to accept office. Instead, remaining as the President of the Congress, he continued to expound his theme of complete independence in innumerable statements and messages, pointing out that the pseudo-democracy under executive vetoes would soon evaporate. The British-sponsored illusion was soon shattered as the Congress ministries were arbitrarily dismissed two years later when they become too inconvenient for the British government in India. The Congress was once again driven to Jawaharlal's two-decade-old unqualified demand for complete independence.

Eighteen Months in India presents a new aspect of Jawaharlal, that of a literary critic. In responding to various criticisms of his thoughts and ideas, Jawaharlal wrote a few critical essays, "To my Friends and Critics," "An Author Replies," "A Roadside Interlude," and "A Question of Manners." In these essays he demonstrated his capacity to be an adept in fencing with journalists, reviewers, and critics without displaying ill-will. Writing in measured ease and at times even counterposing their arguments with weightier criticisms of his own, all in good humor, Jawaharlal appears to have enjoyed his duel in words as much as he dreamed of fighting with a sword in hand. "To newspapers and journalists my gratitude is infinite for their courtesy in giving publicity to what I say and write. Especially I am beholden to my critics who labour so hard to improve me by pointing out my innumerable failings and blemishes. I value that criticism more even than the praise of others." Being a public person, he was aware whatever he said was "news." Yet what amused him was how the casual words from his lips "move people so much, even though sometimes that movement may be one of wrath!" (p. 9).

IV   The Unity of India

The Unity of India, edited by V. K. Krishna Menon with the sub-title, "Collected Writings, 1937–40," contains twelve articles and a pamphlet already published; five speeches, eight travel accounts, twenty-six statements on various matters, and Jawaharlal's statement in the court at his eighth trial on November 3, 1940. Eight of the articles, first published as a series in the *National Herald* of Lucknow and later as a pamphlet, *Where are We?* (p. 84), appear under the caption, "A Survey of Congress Politics, 1936–39." Three other articles were published abroad: "The Unity of India," the title article, in the *Foreign Affairs* (January 1938); "India's Demand and England's Answer" in the *Atlantic Monthly* (January 1940); "The Betrayal of Czechoslovakia" in the *Manchester Guardian* (September 1938). Of the five speeches, three were delivered in India on the subjects of Congress politics, and science and progress; two in Europe in July 1938: "Peace and Empire" the Presidential address delivered at the Peace Conference held in London, "The Bombing of Open Towns," at the International Peace Congress in Paris. The remainder of the writings relate to events in India.

The selections are thematically arranged giving the impression of a studied approach of the editor in presenting the material with a definite purpose in mind, namely to indicate the unity of India at a time when the British government was balking on the question of Indian independence under the excuse that there was disunity in the colony.

Jawaharlal was fortunate in having V. K. Krishna Menon as his editor. By that time Menon had already established himself and the India League in London as a formidable voice of colonial India in the heart of the empire, to the very annoyance and sometimes to the embarrassment of the British government. But Menon was ingenious enough to enlist about a hundred members of the British Parliament in the India League to protect it from the imperial wrath. Besides, by his active involvement in the civic work in the city of London, the Indian colonial subject had become the distinguished Councillor of the Borough of St. Pancreas; he had also gained the support of many progressive, liberal, socialist, and labor leaders of England. Further, Menon had challenged the conservative publishing world of London by assuming the editorship of an innovative, though at that time doubtful, venture, a new series of paperbacks under the name Penguin Books, which was later to revolutionize the book industry. For a young Indian who was born in Kozhikode (Calicut), Malabar in 1897 (eight years after Jawaharlal), who went to England as a student in 1925 on a Y.M.C.A. scholarship, a nonentity who became the Secretary of the India League in 1928, a Dravidian who became a politician extraordinary in the land of the Druids, this was a phenomenal success and unequalled achievement in the imperial capital.

When Jawaharlal visited Europe in 1935, he was impressed by Menon's singular devotion to India's cause and his vigorous campaign in London. Jawaharlal saw in this apparatus a possibility of counteracting the imperial government's resolve to hold unchecked to the colonies, by influencing liberal and progressive leaders in the British Parliament and public life. For the Indian revolution embarked on a nonviolent course, the mental conversion of the legislators of the British Parliament seemed a very scientific approach to the problem, which would finally usher in the Indian independence with honor. Jawaharlal who was then the President of the Indian National Congress appointed Menon as its official representative in Europe with headquarters in London. In this enhanced capacity Menon continued his work of the India League, even when Indian leaders were imprisoned in India, and participated at the International Peace Conference in Brussels in 1936. That Conference was convened to consider an alternative to the League of Nations which had failed to prevent aggression, and grant self-rule to the colonies. Jawaharlal highly appreciated Menon's work, especially at Brussels where Jawaharlal himself had participated in the Congress of Oppressed Nationalities in 1927. Menon's brilliant report on the work of the

Conference and in the cause of Indian independence was com-
mended by Jawaharlal to the Indian National Congress at its Faizpur
session in December 1936.[1]

Before leaving Europe, Jawaharlal entrusted to Menon, "the task
of making the necessary selections of his writings and putting them
together for the publisher" (p. vi). However, when the manuscript
was finally put together, Menon had no opportunity to consult the
author or to show him any proofs because of Jawaharlal's imprisonment (p. iv).

The editor points out that *The Unity of India* is not a "Nehru Scrap
Book" but a helpful guide to point out some of the tragic errors in the
British colonial policy which was contradictory to the principles of
democracy professed in England, and to awaken the moral instinct
in the British public to appreciate the struggle of a reawakening old
nation, India. The collected writings, Menon pointed out, share with
the *Autobiography*, "the outstanding qualities of powerful writing,
historical perspective, consistency of thought, and sense of social
reality" (p. v).

Most of the writings and statements included in *The Unity of India*
relate to the constitutional impasse created by Britain by drafting a
constitution for India in London in the *Government of India Act* of
1935, without consultation with the Indian people, and attempting
to impose it on the colony. This pretentious constitution provided
some form of visible provincial autonomy with invisible absolute
control by British governors, while at the centre it proposed to establish a federal structure with overwhelming power to the empire-
supporting Indian feudal chiefs, landlords, and British industrial
monopolies. Since the Congress was unable to avoid the imposition
of the provincial autonomy in the British format, it contested the
elections in February 1937 and won major victories.

When the Congress decided to accept office and form ministries,
Jawaharlal preferred to remain as the President of the Congress. He
warned the nation that the policy of the Congress should be to beat
the British in their own constitutional game by getting into the legis-
latures; they should strive to scrap the "slave constitution" and vote
for the Constituent Assembly to be elected on the basis of adult
franchise. The selections included in this volume under Part I, "India
and the States" and Part II, "Congress Politics," deal mainly with
these problems.

Among his writings included in Part III, "Away from Politics" are
some delightful personal essays on travel, undertaken partly on Con-

gress work, and at times for escape from his office and politics. He spent two weeks in November–December 1937 in eastern India, traveling through the Surma and the Brahmaputra valleys. While inquiring about the Congress's organizations in that region, he was surprised to learn about the conditions of people in the hills of Assam, which were declared by the British as "excluded areas" and were forbidden to Indian journalists, labor union leaders, social workers and Congress volunteers. The British government had secretly allowed the British tea planters the exclusive use of the unhampered "slave labour" by declaring the region as "excluded areas." Jawaharlal was pained to see the hypocrisy in the loud British propaganda about the Soviet forced labor. While in the Soviet Union the Soviet laborer ultimately would benefit by forced labor, in India the result of the slave labor of the Assamese people, went to enrich England; the British tea companies were robbing India of its richest export by their tea monopoly in the world market (p. 185). He also learned that with the connivance of the British colonial government, the British tea companies "paid exceedingly little in the way of revenue to the State for the land occupied by them. They pay far less than the ordinary agriculturist" while making enormous profits (p. 197). Similarly, "the oil wealth of India was pumped out of Digboi," while Assam and India were deprived of the royalties income under arrangements agreed upon by the British colonial government and the oil monopoly of Burmah Shell (p. 198). The British government issued licenses liberally in the region for growing opium in abundance, and was clandestinely engaged in a profitable drug-pushing trade (p. 191). With all these revelations about the unpleasant economic aspects of the British colonial rule and exploitation, Jawaharlal mused about the "good work" Britain was doing in India!

These revelations were only incidental during Jawaharlal's journeys. He was more delighted by the people of those green valleys who came to see him with affection: "Gatherings of people at small stations, and many tribal folk with gracious gifts of fruit and flowers and cloth, woven by themselves, and fresh milk came to welcome me. Bright-eyed Naga children gave me garlands to wear. Some of these tribal people pressed some money on me also, coppers and nickel coins, for Congress work, they said. And I felt shamed and humbled before their clear gaze, full of faith and affection" (pp. 184–85).

In Bhanubil Jawaharlal saw the Manipur people "extraordinarily neat and clean-looking, and the young girls, with the laughter lurking in their eyes, had quite a smart modern look" (p. 187). These peasant folk with no or little education, good spinners and weavers, took pride in themselves. All these people told him stories of their life-struggle and their sufferings; their efforts during the Gandhian noncooperation days, and the "galling restrictions they suffered under the British rule" with no avenues open for redress.

Behind all these people of the hills and their ruthless colonial administrators and exploiters, there was the landscape itself which Jawaharlal could not help observing. Musing in his own whimsical way, he arrived at the philosophical question as to the meaning of life between nature's domain and civilization's endless strife:

The call of the jungle and the mountain has always been strong with me, a dweller of cities and of plains though I am, and I gazed at these forests and jungles, fascinated, and wondered what myriad forms of life and what tragedy they hid in their darknesses. Bountiful nature, or nature red in tooth and claw— was it much worse in these forest recesses than in the cities and the dwelling places of men and women? A wild animal kills for food to satisfy his hunger. He does not kill for sport or for the pleasure of killing. The fierce fights of the jungle are individual fights, not the mass murder that man calls war. There is no wholesale destruction by bomb and poison gas. The comparison seemed to be all in favour of the forest and the wild animals. (p. 184)

During March–April 1938, Jawaharlal spent another spell of a two-week holiday in the foothills of the Himalayas in his own province, to which experience he gave lyrical expression in another essay, "Escape" (pp. 200–204). In this dramatic monologue, Jawaharlal the romantic is revealed without his political mask. In various thoughts and moods in the company of snow-capped mountains and wind blowing through the pines, Jawaharlal sees himself as struggling in the rut of habit as a politician and wanting to escape to some far-off place. Oscillating between the life-sensation of nature and the dream-sensation of man in society, Jawaharlal achieves a marvelous glimpse of the truth in discovering, like Arjuna in the battle field of Kurukshetra, that there is no escape in the plains, or in the cities, or in the mountains, except perhaps, "to some extent, in action" (p. 204).

In another trip to the foothills of the Himalayas during the first week of May 1938, Jawaharlal traveled by plane, car, horse and on foot. But he seems to have enjoyed the ride on horse and the walk on the foot. When they were at the source of the sacred Ganga, "the river that has held India's heart captive for so many thousand years" he saw weary pilgrims trudging slowly on foot, "their living faith making light of their burdens and their sufferings" (p. 206).

In a long essay "Kashmir" Jawaharlal describes his twelve-day trip to that beautiful valley and the neighboring mountains in July 1940. "In prison or outside," he wrote, "Kashmir haunted me." After twenty-three years of political struggle and many imprisonments, he was back in the land of his ancestors. He was fascinated by the supremely subdued enchantment of the valley which he thought was "like the face of the beloved that one sees in a dream and that fades away on awakening" (p. 223).

In these nonpolitical essays one could see Jawaharlal the aesthete expressing yet another aspect of his rounded personality. He had enjoyed traveling in his school days in India and Europe. He had also read and enjoyed many books on travel and adventure and developed a fascination for the distant and the faraway. For the sense of adventure be it the adventure with idea, or in the panoramic view of the past, or in the landscape of the living present, Jawaharlal seems to be echoing the dictum of his own philosophy of life: Voyage forward adventurer!

The overwhelming spirit of the book is conveyed in the title article, "The Unity of India" (pp. 11–26). Though the article was addressed to Americans, Jawaharlal argues the case of India before the larger audience of the world, including some Anglicized Indians who had soaked up some of the British prejudices about India. People bred even in democratic tradition, Jawaharlal noted, like any other people, have developed unconciously some vague superstitions that one nation means one language, one religion, and one way of life. Jawaharlal considered this notion dangerous, undemocratic in a broad sense, and essentially exhibiting intolerance. On account of this superstition Britain and many other countries were expressing the platitude that because of the "seemingly infinite diversity that makes the fabric of Indian life" independence was not good for India, for it will not "stand together and free, if the British rule were withdrawn" (p. 11).

Jawaharlal rejected this argument as selfish and fallacious; it was advanced by Britain only to evade the question of Indian independence and to support its own "power vacuum" theory. If British fears were genuine, Jawaharlal rebutted, it only demonstrated the way of British perplexity rather than understanding of the Indian situation, even after a hundred years of "unchecked despotic domination."

The unity of a nation, Jawaharlal argued, need not necessarily be in one single factor, like language, race or religion, though these are contributing elements in that unity. The either-or phraseology and the tower of babel imagery may be the particular inhibitions of the Semitic and European traditions. They are totally out of context and irrelevant in a tradition which is rooted in the Upanishadic concept of "unity in rich diversity," exemplified in the expression of a multi-foliate culture drawing on the imagery of the petals of the lotus (pp. 241–42). There is no either-or contradiction among the petals of the same flower.

Until the advent of modern methods of communication and transportation, Jawaharlal pointed out, it was difficult to hold together politically for long the peoples of a vast region. Yet from the earliest times in history attempts were made to establish regional political unity in Asia and in the Mediterranean. In *Glimpses of World History*, Jawaharlal had examined this concept of overall sovereignty in terms of the universal emperor as the son of Heaven in China; the *chakravarti-raja* or the ruler of the world under the symbol of the wheel, in India; or Caesar in Rome. The concept of *chakravarti-raja* connoting a political commonwealth of kingdoms, without economic colonialism was as ancient as Chakravarti-raja Bharata (whose name has become identical with the sub-Himalayan region as "Bharatavarsa") and his descendant, Yudhishthira, the eldest of the Pandavas in the *Mahabharata*. In historic times, after Alexander's raid into the Punjab in 326 B.C., Buddhist Chakravarti-raja Asoka (274–34 B.C.) renouncing violence after winning the Kalinga war, established a unified rule in the Indian subcontinent, including Afghanistan and regions of central Asia, under Buddha's gospel of compassion and nonviolence (unknown of any other ruler in the world). Even Europe-oriented historian like H. G. Wells in his *Outlines of World History* acknowledges Asoka, "the beloved of the gods" as unique among world emperors. The political unity of India was established more than two thousand years ago, when Britain was inhabited by Celtic tribes and was later, reduced to a Roman colony.

Yet Jawaharlal argued, the idea of the political unity of India persisted and other rulers since Asoka tried to achieve it and succeeded in some measure. In this long and continuous tradition of thousands of years, the British colonial rule was only a marginal encroachment, which synchronized with the developments in arms, methods of transport, and communication on account of industrialization. The unity imposed on India either by the East India Company or later by the British colonial rule was the unity of occupation, a unity of common subjugation, common exploitation, and common suffering (p. 19). What is far more important to see, Jawaharlal emphasized, is what other more basic unifying features there are in Indian life.

During India's long course, innumerable people—nomads, settlers, soldiers, scholars, pilgrims, students, merchants, missionaries, predators, and refugees—have trekked into the land, and have influenced Indian life, culture and art. But they always have been absorbed and assimilated: "Like the ocean she received the tribute of a thousand rivers . . . and the sea continued to be the sea" (p. 14). This was possible because of the fundamental cultural attitude; there was no room for an exclusive or intolerant ideology, no Wars of the Roses, or Crusades to eliminate a racial or religious or ideological group. The culture developed a "beneficent attitude which, secure in its own strength, could afford to be tolerant and broadminded. And this toleration gave it its greatest strength and adaptability" (p. 15). As against this tolerant approach, Jawaharlal suggests, "it is interesting to compare the intolerance of Europe." The pre-Christian European culture was castigated as pagan; the Protestant and Catholic controversies within a creed led to massacres, wars, persecution and even genocide of another Semitic religious group. India on the other hand accommodated, besides its own religions three Semitic religions—Judaism in the fourth century B.C., Christianity in the first century A.D. and Islam in the ninth century A.D.—and the Zoroastrian religion in the seventh century A.D.. It was only when the militant Islam of the Afghans and the Moghuls, and the militant Christianity of Europe, backed by occupation armies, swords, guns and bombs, came to the land, more greedy for the riches of the land than any intent of serving the spirit, that conflicts arose with foreign religions and their cultures. Yet the Indian spirit of synthesis overcame these conflicts in the long run.

A possible key to this assimilation, Jawaharlal points out, is the Upanishadic rationalism requiring "ceaseless attempts to find harmony between the inner man and his outer environment" (p. 17). When this rationalism became clouded by superstition and dogma, revolutionary leaders like Buddha in the sixth century B.C., Shankara in the seventh century A.D. and Bhaktas in the thirteenth and four-teenth centuries A.D., and Mahatma Gandhi in the twentieth century labored to restore that "mental atmosphere of the country," in which various groups were once again able to see the petals and the unity of the lotus. It was during those periods when the mental atmosphere of the country changed from dynamic to static condition that India fell an easy prey to aggressors, and it was during one of such periods of weakness and decay within India that the British adventurers grad-ually crept from the shores of the land as harmless merchants to the heights of the Himalayas as arrogant imperialists (p. 18).

But the tide had changed, Jawaharlal was convinced, and India was seeking to reassert that Upanishadic mental atmosphere of the country and the vivid perception of the unity of the nation. In this process the nation had to overcome hindrances imposed by the Brit-ish during their colonial rule mainly to create Indian support for the empire, in the freezing of the medieval society, in the reinforcement of the feudal economy and institutions, in the deliberate prevention of the industrial growth, absence of mass education, the mortgaging of Indian income to London bankers and British monopolies, and the recent attempt to impose a constitution meant to sustain these obstacles (pp. 19–23). To illustrate his own conviction of the unity of India, Jawaharlal quoted a Brahmanized Briton, Sir Frederick Whyte who had come to sense this pervasive presence of the unity of the lotus: "The greatest of all the contradictions in India is that over this diversity is spread a greater unity, which is not immediately evident because it failed historically to find expression, in any po-litical cohesion to make the country one, but which is so great a reality, and so powerful that even the Moslem world in India has to confess that it has been deeply affected by coming within its influence."[2]

The fallacy of the British attitude, Jawaharlal argued, is that In-dians converted to Islam or European Christianity do not become Arabs or Europeans even though they slavishly imitate their outward ways of life. It was only under the benign imperial encouragement that Muhammad Iqbal and Muhammad Jinnah hoisted the medieval Arabian theological point of view that Islam cannot live with any other religion, and therefore Indian Muslims cannot live in peace with the rest of the religions in India. The very partition proved the falsity of this archaic dogma inasmuch as some sixty million Muslims swallowing this slogan had to stay in non-Islamic India, and they were not worse off for that.[3]

Concluding his long thesis, Jawaharlal stated that the view of the unity of India was not uniquely his own but was shared by many men and leaders of India who had vision to see, by men who led the Indian National Congress during the years, in spite of their professing different faiths; all of them saw the unity of the nation in the total culture. Only when the imperial outside power with its Machiavellian policies ceased to meddle in the affairs of India, Jawaharlal emphasized, would the nation easily come to realize its fundamental unity.

This forceful statement was a daring assertion of the perception of the historical situation as Jawaharlal looked on the nation's suffering. He continued his examination of the unity of the nation later in his more profound work *The Discovery of India*.

CHAPTER 8

Search for Identity:
The Discovery of India (*1946*)

I *Last Imprisonment*

IN his preface to *The Discovery of India*, Jawaharlal states, "This book was written by me in Ahmadnagar Fort Prison during the five months, April to September, 1944" (p. vii). Then he was imprisoned by the British government for the ninth time, his longest term (1041 days) and the last. On similar previous occasions he had written the *Glimpses of World History* in fifteen months and *An Autobiography* in eight months. Apparently, Jawaharlal, the prison-author, had achieved in the course of his imprisonments progressive concentration in writing so that he wrote his *Discovery* in five months out of the three years he was in prison.

Jawaharlal's ninth detention was without the usual farce of court trial. He was simply arrested and sent to jail with thousands of others. From the British point of view that was a short cut to their security. When war was declared in Europe in September 1939, Britain felt her empire was threatened not so much from outside as from within. The Indian National Congress was demanding a categorical promise of independence as a price for cooperation with the British in their war effort. The Congress was well aware of earlier British vague promise of self-rule in 1915 and its negation after the war. In spite of this unheroic precedent, Britain wanted Indian resources and men to fight her European war without her being willing to give that same freedom to Indians which she was trying to preserve for herself in Europe. Instead Britain unilaterally committed India as a belligerent country on her side. The Congress protested at this maneuver, and Gandhi launched the "symbolic Satyagraha," or public anti-war protests by selected individuals. In response, the British government arrested and imprisoned Congress leaders, whether they made such protest speeches or not. Jawaharlal was arrested on October 31, 1940, and sentenced to four years rigorous imprisonment in Gorakhpur prison, six days prior to the day he was scheduled to speak!

Under the pressure of war, the British government changed its mind and released all the symbolic Satyagrahis. Along with other Congress leaders, Jawaharlal was released on December 3, 1941. Though Gandhi had not suspended his movement, he advised Congressmen who wanted to offer themselves again as symbolic Satyagrahis to withhold their protests for some time, giving the British government time to come to some terms. This Gandhian restraint unfortunately was misconstrued by the colonial officials as weakness in the Congress on account of the controversy that was going on at that time on the issue of nonviolence and the support for the British war effort.

Japan's entry into the war in the Asian theatre impelled Britain once again to conciliate the Congress with a view to securing Indian cooperation to defend her empire in Asia. The Congress demanded the formation of a national government with the British Viceroy remaining as the constitutional head, but the Viceroy and Britain insisted on retaining complete control and opposed the transfer of power. The failure of these renewed negotiations under Gandhi's patiently pursued policy, aggravated the situation. At the same time, Britain's establishments in Southeast Asia were falling into the Japanese hands. In their utter despair the British officials followed a scorched earth policy of destroying material and human resources before they fell to the enemy. The ruthless horror of this policy became real when eastern India was subjected to it and thousands of people in Bengal and Orissa were killed, some made destitute, their crops destroyed, houses burned, and the masses deprived of their means of livelihood.

Gandhi was aghast at this wanton destruction and burning of India and its people, not by the so-called "enemy" but by the imperial trustee and lawgiver, Britain. In his anguish Gandhi called upon the bedeviled British to "Quit India" instead of burning her food crops and shooting her people, making them destitute, and subjecting them to more cruel misery. If the British refused, he wanted the Congress to launch a full scale noncooperation movement against a nonresponsive government. When Gandhi's famous "Quit India" resolution was adopted by the Congress in Bombay on August 8, 1942, the British government rushed in the early hours of August 9, to arrest all the important leaders gathered in Bombay, thereafter declaring the Congress illegal, imprisoning Congress workers throughout the country. Thousands of Congress leaders were arrested and imprisoned without trial. Jawaharlal was arrested at dawn on August 9 in Bombay and imprisoned in Ahmadnagar Fort Prison. While Britain took proper care of European prisoners of war detained in India, especially those from Italy and Germany, at India's expense under the Geneva Convention, Britain with impunity treated political Indian prisoners badly. For the Geneva Convention did not apply to freedom struggles, if such wars took place in European colonies (p. 2).

Jawaharlal was detained in Ahmadnagar Fort Prison from August 9, 1942 until March 28, 1945; thereafter he was transferred to Naini Gaol, Bareilley Gaol, and then to Almora Gaol from which he was released on June 15, 1945. Though Jawaharlal was in prison at Ahmadnagar for two years and seven months, *The Discovery of India* was written during a brief period, June to September 1944. What was he doing for over a year and eight months before he commenced writing, or during six months after he stopped writing? For the first twenty months of his imprisonment, Jawaharlal states, "I have often thought of writing, felt the urge to it and at the same time a reluctance." Yet he did not write for "there was a certain distaste for just throwing out a book which had no particular significance" (p. 23). Instead he took to gardening "and spent many hours daily, even when the sun was hot, in digging and preparing beds for flowers" (p. 25). In this process he struggled with mother earth trying to unravel the mystery of Mother India. And twenty-one months was a long time for digging when each day in prison was of the same monotonous duration. When once he started writing in April 1944, he was progressing at the average and withal brisk speed of seven pages a day in long hand, and that too by managing to secure the paper with "considerable difficulty." After nearly five months had passed, and when he had "covered a thousand hand written pages" with the jumble of ideas in his mind, he had "exhausted his limited supply of paper" and his narrative came to an end for this "very practical consideration" (p. 686).

Jawaharlal did not want to write just another book, or any book which would grow stale while he sat in prison with his manuscript and the world went on changing; nor did he desire to write something that was meant to be a continuation of his autobiography (p. 24).

Consequently, the reason why he wrote, and the circumstances of his writing become crucial to the understanding of what he actually wrote in *The Discovery of India.*

II *Scholarly Company*

Even though Jawaharlal was imprisoned, was digging the inexhaustible earth, and searching within the wilderness of his spirit as a private penance, he was cast in the company of eleven distinguished scholars as fellow-prisoners. From their discussions and mental stimulation Jawaharlal's mind was saturated.

My eleven companions in Ahmadnagar Fort were an interesting cross-section of India and represented in their several ways not only politics but Indian scholarship, old and new, and various aspects of present-day India. Nearly all the principle living Indian languages, as well as the classical languages which have powerfully influenced India in the past and present, were represented and the standard was often that of high scholarship. Among the classical languages were Sanskrit and Pali, Arabic and Persian; the modern languages were Hindi, Urdu, Bengali, Gujarati, Marathi, Telugu, Sindhi and Oriya. I had all this wealth to draw upon and the only limitation was my own capacity to profit by it. Though I am grateful to all my companions, I should like to mention especially Maulana Abul Kalam Azad, whose vast erudition invariably delighted me but sometimes also rather overwhelmed me, Govind Ballabh Pant, Narendra Deva and M. Asaf Ali. (p. vii)

This intellectual aristocracy in the prison of real men of flesh and bone did not become fictionalized in Jawaharlal's work, like the ducal assembly of the learned in the Italian Renaissance classic, Castiglione's *The Courtier*. Instead their composite culture had an unmistakable impact on Jawaharlal's writings, giving it scholarly depth, a wide variety of sophistication, and, above all, a disciplined presentation of the material in organized chapters, with subsections. Each of these subsections can be considered as a well developed essay bearing the imprint of considerable scholarship and aesthetic sensibility, grouped under related chapters. The book has the appearance of a report of a group workshop, galvanized by its indefatigable spokesman, Jawaharlal. Appropriately, he dedicated his work "To my Colleagues and Co-prisoners in the Ahmadnagar Fort Prison Camp from August 9, 1942 to March 28, 1945." Thus, it appears, what was reduced to writing in Jawaharlal's longhand had gone through the mill of their collective minds and sieved through Jawaharlal's own matured being.

In his preface written in December 29, 1945, almost a year and a quarter after he finished writing the book, Jawaharlal recognized that "some parts of it" relating to contemporary events "are already somewhat out of date," and much has happened since then. Though he felt tempted to add and revise, he found himself confronted with a "different texture" of life outside prison, which gave him no leisure for thought and writing. He was then involved in the making of history and forming the nucleus of the interim government of India. In his preoccupation with the national affairs, he regretted, he was "unable to find time to read the typescript" until Indira came to his rescue and took over that burden from his shoulders. Consequently, the book remains "as written in prison with no additions or changes except for the postscript at the end."

Why did Jawaharlal find it difficult to get into the mood and emotion of his book outside the prison? Why was the texture of life different? With the remarkable self-analysis of a literary critic, Jawaharlal lays bare like a Buddhist divine the shreds of a writer's personality, continually changing like a flame, yet holding on to an apparent unity, and continually giving light from its intense activity. The flame that burnt at the first instant is not the same flame that burns at a later instant. So also the author who conceives in his mind and as he feeds those concepts with his vision and emotions and thoughts, delivers his work in progress. Can he relive that process? Can an artist ever reenter his work in the same spirit? Says Jawaharlal:

I do not know how other authors feel about their writings but always I have a strange sensation when I read something that I had written some time previously. That sensation is heightened when the writing had been done in the close and abnormal atmosphere of prison and the subsequent reading has taken place outside. I recognize it of course, but not wholly; it seems almost that I was reading some familiar piece written by another, who was near to me and yet who was different. Perhaps that is the measure of the change that has taken place in me.

So I have felt about this book also. It is mine and not wholly mine, as I am constituted today; it represents rather some past self of mine which has already joined that long succession of other selves that existed for a while and faded away, leaving only a memory behind. (p. viii)

III *India Through the Ages*

The Discovery of India contains ten chapters, a two-page post-script, and a short preface, both dated December 29, 1945. Each chapter carrying a heading, contains a number of titled subsections, ranging from six to twenty-one. If each subsection could be read as a short essay, then the book contains 127 essays arranged under ten major headings in about seven hundred printed pages.

The book begins and ends in Ahmadnagar Fort Prison, discussing current reality in India and the world. Chapter 2, is rather unusual and apart in the sense it reminisces Kamala in six essays when she was in Badenweiler and Lausanne from September 1935 to March 1936, and Jawaharlal's return to India with an urn containing her ashes and their dissolution in the sacred Ganga. Chapter 3, "The Quest" examines in ten essays the concept of "India" from the peasant's and from the sophisticated person's points of view and sets the search. The next three chapters discuss India's history, culture and traditions: chapter 4, "The Discovery of India" (twenty-one essays), traces the story of the Dravido-Aryan civilization from the Indus Valley to the time of Asoka; chapter 5, "Through the Ages," (twenty-one essays) continues the story further to the end of the classical period in about 1000 A.D., including some consideration of diverse cultural contributions and Indian cultural expansion into other parts of Asia; chapter 6, "New Problems" (sixteen essays) discusses foreign incursions into India and the impact of two Semitic religions, Islam and Christianity; the invasion by the Moghuls from the north and the British from the south in the sixteenth century, and their successive establishment of empires. The remaining three chapters (7–9) all titled, "The Last Phase," with varying subheadings, deal with nineteenth- and twentieth-century India: Consolidation of the British Rule and the Rise of Nationalist Movement, twelve essays; Nationalism versus Imperialism, eight essays; and World War II, ten essays (the last essay discussing the "Quit India" Resolution of August 8, 1942). The postscript brings the story up to date from March 1945, the time Jawaharlal left Ahmadnagar Fort Prison until the end of the year.

Obviously, *The Discovery of India* contains restatement of some material from Jawaharlal's earlier works, especially, *Glimpses of World History* and *An Autobiography*, but this is refined through the crucible of the critical apparatus of the prison workshop of scholars, and Jawaharlal's own mellowed viewpoint. Much of the cultural material on India has arrived through the translations in the *Sacred Books of the East* series edited by F. Max Muller and the Oriental scholarship of European and Asian scholars which are acknowledged through footnotes. Nevertheless, this material is synthesized in Jawaharlal's smithy and what is presented is a panoramic view of Indian civilization as seen, somewhat unconventionally through the eyes of an Indian freedom fighter. In this sense the book is a personalized history, Jawaharlal's supreme *bhashya* or the crystallization of his life-long commentary on the amorphous idea of present-day India as variously understood by different peoples of the sub-Himalayan region as Dravida-nadu, Jambhu-dwipa, Bharat Mata, Bharat-varsa, Sindu, Hindu, Indos, or Hindustan.

IV   *The Lady with a Past*

Even though the first and the tenth chapters are entitled "Ahmadnagar Fort Prison" and to some extent relate a few personal details (and there are other personal references throughout the narrative), the only chapter which is wholly autobiographical is the second chapter, entitled, "Badenweiler: Lausanne" (pp. 29–40), and devoted to Kamala, his wife, who was taken to Badenweiler, Germany in May 1935, and who died in Lausanne, Switzerland, on February 28, 1936. By starting his quest with Kamala, Jawaharlal felt he could connect the writer in him to the concluding portion of his earlier sustained work;

I shall begin this story with an entirely personal chapter, for this gives the clue to my mood in the month immediately following the period I had written about towards the end of my autobiography. But this is not going to be an autobiography, though I am afraid the personal element will often be present. (p. 28)

Almost ten years after Kamala's death, Jawaharlal was recalling, in Ahmadnagar Fort Prison, how he shared the last five months of Kamala's life, remembering their long married life of twenty years in which they had very little time to give to each other. In this recollection of recollections Jawaharlal romanticizes his wife and discovers some beautiful gifts she bore as wife and woman, giving meaning to his life. It is not clear why Jawaharlal started on this sentimental journey in *The Discovery of India*. His declared purpose was to get into the mood of writing but it appears that his undeclared reason was that he sought to reinforce his search for identity beginning it with the woman who shared his life, and from that experience of a known woman to know about the woman he was searching to know, Mother India, who had given him his being. In any case, Kamala's shadow was haunting him for a long time and perhaps by writing about her he might have overcome that uneasy feeling. It may have also been Jawaharlal's private excursion into his personal life, escaping from his scholarly company. For his prison loneliness takes him across a time-gap to the period of his lonely days in Badenweiler when he tried to see Kamala in retrospect:

> In the long autumn evenings I sat by myself in my room in the pension, where I was staying, or sometimes went out for a walk across the fields or through the forest. A hundred pictures of Kamala succeeded each other in my mind, a hundred aspects of her rich and deep personality. We had been married for nearly twenty years and yet how many times she had surprised me by something new in her mental or spiritual make-up. I had known her in so many ways and, in later years, I had tried my utmost to understand her. That understanding had not been denied to me, but I often wondered if I really knew her or understood her. There was something elusive about her, something fay-like, real but unsubstantial, difficult to grasp. Sometimes, looking into her eyes, I would find a stranger peeping out at me. (p. 30)

Kamala would still be peeping out at him then across the gap of living and nonliving, or living in another form, for he felt within him rather acutely that by "giving himself utterly to the cause" of national independence, he "almost forgot her and denied her in many ways that comradeship which was her due" (p. 31). Yet Jawaharlal and even his father Motilal, were proud of her as she got herself involved in the Congress work on her own, and even got herself arrested and imprisoned for the sake of Mother India and for her freedom. In spite of all these heroic attitudes, Kamala was still a woman, and Jawaharlal recalls her premonitions at the time of their last normal parting in their house when Jawaharlal was arrested on February 14, 1934:

> When I was arrested in February 1934 on a Calcutta warrant, Kamala went up to our rooms to collect some clothes for me. I followed her to say good-bye to her. Suddenly she clung to me, and fainting, collapsed. This was unusual

for her as we had trained ourselves to take this jail-going lightly and cheer-
fully and to make as little fuss about it as possible. Was it some premonition
she had that this was our last more or less normal meeting? (p. 34)

Perhaps this lady from Kashmir "with little schooling" but a
large heart saw the reality of the end of their journey together under
normal circumstances. Thereafter, she was not her own self but was
taken from sanitorium to sanitorium in India and in Europe. Her
death came almost as a relief but it left Jawaharlal with a haunting
memory.

When Kamala's ashes were poured into the "bosom of that noble
river" Ganges there was the dissolution of the woman he knew into
the woman he was yet to know. Like Dante's Dona Portinari who
as Beatrice became the leading lady of the poet for his voyage of
discovery through the *Divine Comedy*, so also in Jawaharlal's epic
quest Kamala, the "red lotus" of love from Kashmir is "glimpsed"
in infinitely varying Upanishadic imageries as the symbol of *dharma*
(law), as Buddha's *saddharma pundarika* (law of the lotus of the
heart), until she becomes indistinguishably dissolved with the dissolution of her ashes in the bosom of the Ganges whose waters
millions have embraced in the past, and millions yet to come will
embrace in the future (p. 40). Thus as he was digging mother earth
in order to make a flower bed, in his memory this "lady with a past"
having that "illusive quality of a legend of long ago" became none
other than Mother India. Unlike the Dantean or Freudian psychic
complex, this is more in keeping with Bhakti and Tantric tradition
of fulfillment of one's quest in the person of a woman as a giver of
life, love, and liberation, or Lao Tzu's "the spirit of the valley." It
is no wonder that Jawaharlal, the man of action, who was wedded
to the cause of the freedom of India found in this metamorphosis
his *sat-chit-ananda* (the joy that comes from the realization of truth)
in his *Discovery of India*.

V *Writer and his Craft*

Having written so much about world history already, one may
wonder why Jawaharlal chose once again to write about Indian
history, even though it was a personalized account. He had dis-
claimed himself as being a historian; nor was he qualified or trained
to write history. Yet whatever he wrote, in the main, was nothing
but historical or history in the making, in the immediate context

of his experience. In an essay "The Burden of the Past" (p. 23–28), Jawaharlal in explaining the reason for writing on history also gives another marvelous exposé of himself as a writer, and a unique self-criticism on a writer and his craft in terms of three perspectives: the present, the future and the past.

Jawaharlal was as much a man of action as he was a man of thought, and as such he was the man of the present. He felt he could best express himself in action and reflection thereon: "I cannot write about the present so long as I am not free to experience it through action. It is the need for action in the present that brings it vividly to me, and then I can write about it with ease and a certain facility" (p. 26). When that present and the opportunity for action were denied to him, he felt he was cut off from the real experience. For in prison it was something vague, shadowy, something he could not come to grips with or experience as the sensation of the moment. It ceased to be the present for him in any real sense, yet it was not the past either. In this state of limbo he felt he was not living nor could he write.

On the other hand, the future was open. He had often foreseen consequences of actions and warned about the dangers rather accurately. That was when he was in the middle of action. But in his forced isolation he felt he could not assume the role of a prophet and write about the future: "My mind often thinks of it and tries to pierce its veil and clothe it in the garments of my choice." But these are vain imaginings and the "future remains uncertain, unknown, and there is no assurance that it will not betray again our hopes and prove false to humanity's dreams" (p. 26).

The only choice that was left to a man of action isolated in a prison and refusing to speculate about the future, was to write about the past. But the past as academic history was too dry and did not interest him, unless it dissolved in the present, and merged with his life, thought and feelings, and became one with him in the living present. This metabolism of history into the lifeblood of a man making history, he explains, drove him into the unresisting necessity to express and re-express the past as he saw it, over and over again, every time with some different thrill and excitement:

The past remains. But I cannot write academically of past even in the manner of a historian or scholar. I have not that knowledge or equipment or training; nor do I possess the mood for that kind of work. The past oppresses me or fills me sometimes with its warmth when it touches on the present, and becomes, as it were, an aspect of that living present. If it does not do so, then it is cold, barren, lifeless, uninteresting. I can only write about it, as I have previously done, by bringing it in some relation to my present-day thoughts and activities, and then this writing of history, as Goethe once said, brings some relief from the weight and burden of the past. It is, I suppose, a process similar to that of psychoanalysis, but applied to a race or to humanity itself instead of to an individual. (p. 26)

VI *Personal Discovery*

It is in Lao Tzu' sense of "returning to the roots to find peace" that Jawaharlal indulged in his *Discovery of India* to return to his cultural and spiritual roots. It was a kind of Odyssean wandering in search of an ideal civilization, or a pilgrim's progress, or a Dantean descent and ascent for the sake of his lady love. *The Discovery of India* is Jawaharlal's love story, a mature man's romance with ideas, for India was more of a cultural idea than a patch of earth. It was a whole way of living, rooted in the earth nursed by an ever-renewing "mental climate"; it was also the continuing stream of life carrying with it the blessings and curses of the past as its inheritance. For the idea of India that the sophisticated people had and *Bharat Mata* that villagers and millions of the masses understood, included not only all of these notions but more: "India was all this that they had thought, but it was much more. The mountains and the rivers of India, and the forests and the broad fields, which gave us food, were all dear to us, but what counted ultimately were the people of India, people like them and me, who were spread out all over this vast land. *Bharat Mata* was essentially these millions of people and victory to her meant victory to these people" (p. 55).

Consequently, the "Discovery of India" meant the discerning of the living pulse of the people of India as it was beating in the hearts of those who have gone by, as in those that were struggling in the field of the living, and those million others yet to come. It was visualizing this continuing cycle of unending chain of ever-widening stream of consciousness to which Jawaharlal committed himself in his greatest work. Quite appropriately then, in the process of discovering India, in exploring that unfathomable lotus of the heart in that "lady with a past," Mother India, Jawaharlal takes up the lady of his past (to set the mood, the temper and the attitude), Kamala; the traditional symbol of love and the law; and all that is dear in Indian thought and emotion, becomes the starting point of his discovery. As the echo of a vanished form becomes his "om", leading him to journey into the regions of love—love for one person, love of many, love of the nation, and love of its multi-foliate cultural tradition.

In this love conquest, India's past is not history but in the Jungian sense a recollection of "the collective unconscious of the race"[1] in a beautific vision of the *Empireo, the Primum Mobile,* of finding the macrocosm of the nation in the microcosm of the individual, or the realization of the Upanishadic Brahman in the imperishable atman. The concentrated meditation on the atmic gravitation to the supreme self in Laya Yoga is the process of discovering India. It is internal; it is a realization. It is an individual discovery and a personal experience and cannot be communicated.

What about the words then? Thousands and thousands of words that are left behind in an accummulated form, which are printed in a book. What about them? Words are not experiences. Words are shells of thought. They are the lost self of the author and all the lost selves of the race whose collective unconscious becomes reexpressed in words. Words by themselves are nothing. One may read and re-read a mountain of words without realizing the experience which caused their expression. Words hardly package experience; they package limited meaning. They can only suggest or stimulate a similar experience if the reader is willing and in a position to expand his being as elastically as the author, or tune his self to the wavelengths in which the writer radiates his experience in words. Without the same experience, vision, thought, suffering, contact, and stimulation of the author, the reader may not hope to generate in himself even a somewhat parallel experience much less an identical one. To the extent a reader yokes himself to the task of realizing that experience of the author in his own being, he may come to understand the meaning. It is an exercise in the parallel "glimpse" of the reality through the cumulative effect of words and not the achievement of the structural cohesion of words or rather etymological meaning only.

Realizing this ineffableness of his experience, Jawaharlal pointed out that in the mode of his discovery of India, words were only peripheral:

What stand out in my mind are personal experiences which had left their impress upon me; contacts with certain individuals and certain events; contacts with the crowd, the mass of the Indian people, in their infinite diversity and yet their amazing unity; some adventures of the mind; waves of unhappiness and the relief and joy that came from overcoming them; the exhilaration of the moment of action. About much of this one may not write. There is an intimacy about one's inner life, one's feelings and thoughts, which may not and cannot be conveyed to others. Yet those contacts, personal and impersonal, mean much. (pp. 24–25)

In the cultures and traditions that have grown out of the certainty of the logos, or the written word, one could become enslaved by the conceptual reality. But in a tradition that emphasizes "whatever is written is not the truth; and whatever is true is not written," that which is written is less than a fraction of the truth. Perhaps Wu Cheng-en knew better. When Lord Buddha gave the blank scripture to the Monkey he told the seeker that that was the true scripture. But the Monkey could not read that unwritten law and wanted something in writing; so Lord Buddha gave the Monkey a written scripture but warned him that it was not the truth.[2] The usefulness of the written words lies in the realization of its limitation in communicating experience.

VII   *Cultural Identity*

The discovery of one's self or the realization of one's cultural identity is not merely for the sake of discovery; it is not an idle escape; it is for the sake of life and living a better life. It is essentially an ethical and aesthetic discovery of refining one's sensibilities. It is like digging into mother earth, as Jawaharlal did most of the time in his prison, and discovering the nature of the soil, the possibility of making a flower bed, of the beauty that would emerge as life would grow and flowers blossom, helped by the labor of one's own hands, while digging in the earth, and suddenly of finding a relic of the past reminding that life had been there before, and the mother earth sustains them all—the dead, the living, and the unborn, while still digging in the earth. This growing realization while digging in the earth would make the digging more meaningful. It was in this spirit of digging into the inexhaustible past to make flower beds for the future that Jawaharlal started on *Discovery of India*: "I have put away my spade and taken to my pen instead" (p. 25). The experiences of this voyage of discovery though personal, Jawaharlal acknowledges "affect the individual and mould him and change his reactions to life, to his own country, and to other nations" (p. 25). It was in this reintegration of his person and ceasing to become the vehicle of selfish cravings that Jawaharlal sought his nirvana through the pen.

After his intense *tapas* of five long months in Ahmadnagar Fort Prison, and writing over a thousand pages in longhand, what did Jawaharlal discover? The kind of realization that he came to is his own. Yet in a lyrical passage in the epilogue he gives us the impressions of his vision of a woman, Mother India, the "lady with a past":

The Discovery of India—what have I discovered? It was presumptuous of me to imagine that I could unveil her past. Today she is four hundred million separate individual men and women, each differing from the other, each living in a private universe of thought and feeling. If this is so in the present, how much more difficult is it to grasp that multitudinous past of innumerable successions of human beings. Yet something has bound them together and binds them still. India is a geographical and economic entity, a cultural unity amidst diversity, a bundle of contradictions held together by strong but indivisible threads. Overwhelmed again and again, her spirit was never conquered, and today when she appears to be the plaything of a proud conqueror, she remains unsubdued and unconquered. About her there is the illusive quality of a legend of long ago; some enchantment seems to have held her mind. She is a myth and an idea, a dream and a vision, and yet very real and present and pervasive. There are terrifying glimpses of dark corridors which seems to lead back to primeval night, but also there is the fullness and warmth of the day about her. Shameful and repellant she is occasionally, perverse and obstinate, sometimes even a little hysteric, this lady with a past. But she is very lovable and none of her children can forget her wherever they go or whatever strange fate befalls them. . . (pp. 686–87)

The vision becomes the "double-vision" of Arjuna of the *visva-rupa* in the eleventh chapter of the *Bhagavad Gita*. Who can define this fascinating illusion? Though she may change her attire, Jawaharlal notes, she will continue as of old refreshed like the Ushas. Perhaps one could only speak of her in the negative definition of the *Upanishads*, "Neti! Neti!" (Not this, not this).

CHAPTER 9

Conclusion

JAWAHARLAL NEHRU was not a professional author who devoted his lifetime to writing but a man of public affairs who became a writer by necessity. By training he was a scientist and a lawyer; by choice he was a politician; by attitude he was a humanist; and by sensibilities he was a poet. Yet what he wrote was historical prose, or prose that has become historical. His writings were directly related to his life, his life was totally involved in a cause, and that cause was a historical movement. Consequently, it is difficult to disassociate his writings from his actions, and his actions from history. If "the end of all thought is action" Jawaharlal argued, quoting Romain Rolland, he felt in his case, thought was partly expressive action when the possibility of action was denied to him because of imprisonment.[1] Nevertheless, Jawaharlal's works display some marked common characteristics: they are essentially functional writings; they have an overriding historical perspective and contain some philosophic generalizations; while they are endowed with a certain moral earnestness, they are not without the directness of a personal conversational style, at times flowing in rhythmic beauty.

I *Functional Writings*

As he explained, Jawaharlal could only write with facility after experiencing an action.[2] His writings thus become expressive of his feelings, emotions, and thoughts connected with events in national or international life. Whether he issued statements to the press, wrote essays or discussed questions, most of the time his written works were related to historical happenings. On account of this contemporary relevance many of his books could be regarded as occasional writings conditioned by a particular need, and having some topicality. Some of the events about which Jawaharlal wrote, in spite of their contemporary importance, have ceased to exercise the passions of later generations; others have become merely historical; while some others have achieved national or international significance. In Jawaharlal's writings they all become observed once again from an unusual point of view, and even a dull historical event becomes exciting adventure, mainly because he experienced the action as a nationalist and as an internationalist and wrote about it in his own personal way. Even in his autobiography, he maintains, he was not reporting the events as in a chronicle, but simply writing about them as if they were the circumstances in his voyage of adventure. What was written therefore was not about events but their effect on Jawaharlal in a particular state of being, whether inside or outside prison.[3]

On the one hand, Jawaharlal's writings represent his mental development, progressing from Congress worker to international spokesman; they verbalize the catharsis of a politician on a world stage. On the other hand, in his word-pictures Jawaharlal also portrays the great social urges and aspirations of his time, and even the constructive discontent of a gigantic mass of people becomes identified with a vital rebellion of the spirit which was part of Jawaharlal himself and in its transference, of his age. Consequently, modern India has become inseparately intermixed with Jawaharlal Nehru, his life, his works, and his thoughts.

Jawaharlal's functional writings are to be distinguished from the literary works of some socialist writers whose literary output is solely directed toward a social goal, or from the writings of other purposive writers who aim at some social reform. Though independence was the ultimate goal of Jawaharlal, his works were all spontaneous responses to events and situations at the time of their writing, and remain functional on account of the circumstances of their expression.

II *Historical Perspective*

Though most of Jawaharlal's writings were occasioned by contemporary events, what is unmistakable in his books is his overriding historical perspective. He was always conscious that history was not something that was in the past but it was continuous with the present and included the future. Besides he felt that he himself, by his actions and involvement with the cause of freedom, was acting in the context of history and helping to make it. In his view history was not limited to a group of people, or a nation or a cultural community, but history, in its proper sense, meant and included all the peoples of the world. This global view of life and a comparative attitude to the origin, growth, and evolution of various societies, their institutions, religions, ideologies, and visions of welfare in different regions at different times in history, account for Jawaharlal's unconventional point of view. What may look to be terribly important from a tribal or ethnocentric group point of view in Europe or in Asia, may wholly be unimportant from the context of a wider perspective of a cultural community, or may seem even accidental from the viewpoint of the world community as a whole. By distinguishing the perennial elements from the accidentals in history, he magnified these unifying urges of mankind instead of glorifying tribal vanities.

In the circumstances one can understand his stand that he was neither anti-British nor pro-British empire; for he acknowledged that the British nation, which had also contributed to the human culture from which he had derived some benefits, had every right to be free and independent; but he was against British imperialism, as he would be against any other imperialism. Because of the perception of the broad sweeps of world history he was able to make the subtler distinction, and keep it in his mind most of the time during the bitter struggle for Indian freedom against imperial Britain. What makes for the arrogance of the British imperialists, or any other imperialists, in trampling over the freedom of other peoples, Jawaharlal felt, was a malady or a vain conceit in some people of that nation.[4] One cannot treat the sickness by condemning the person, nor can one condemn a nation for the sickness or the ideologic mania of some of its people. Thus Jawaharlal combined his historical perspective with a refreshingly unconventional point of view in dealing with human affairs.

In his story of the early days of the world of "millions of years in the making" and in the story of the many countries into which the world is divided, Jawaharlal sharpened the existentialist's focus on world evolution of human culture. From the historical point of view, the freedom movement was not the cause of the disruption of the so-called British law and order in India, but it was the consequence of a previous cause which subverted freedom in India, namely British aggression and occupation. The undoing of this British violence to the Indian nation was a natural reaction. Consequently, the process of decolonization was a process of helping the British to get rid of their sickness in which they saw a nightmare of the "whiteman's burden" placed upon them, or assumed themselves to be a superior race, or the chosen people or the policeman of the world. By understanding the nature of the British imperial malady and sharing in the suffering of the Indian people, Jawaharlal was able to humanize the freedom struggle, even as he suffered prison life, or when he was being beaten by the English police officer with his imperial baton for carrying the Congress flag, or when he made a statement to the court at his eighth trial in Gorakhpur Prison.

It was because of his historical perspective that Jawaharlal, more than any other leader in India, saw in the contemporary world, movements to change social and economic structures in various societies, and was able to identify the Indian re-awakening and the awakening of other oppressed peoples as a part of the world struggle. While for the British the suppression of the freedom struggle in the colony was an expediency, resistance of that oppression was a vital necessity from the Indian point of view. When one views an event within the limited context of a few years it may appear to be terribly important but when that same event is viewed from the context of a hundred years, or of the long history of the world, it may acquire quite different aspects. It seemed imperative for the Imperial Government to imprison thousands of Indian leaders in their own country, and deny the Indian people their own resources to make a better life. But those who struggled to redeem the oppressor and the oppressed considered their suffering a worthwhile sacrifice in the larger context of history.

This attitude renders Jawaharlal's writings devoid of bitterness; instead it charges them with the sadness of human tears. They lift the reader's perspective to a higher point and make him see the causes and the previous causes of events, and also the possible consequences. In many of his writings, the wisdom of Jawaharlal's warnings on conflicting courses taken by the British or the Congress or by governments in other parts of the world becomes evident. Though not a historican by meticulous collation of facts, Jawaharlal, by developing this historical perspective, was able to sense the pulse of the living movements in history, and also behold glimpses of truth.

III   *Moral Earnestness*

Because of his extended view of life and events on the face of the earth, Jawaharlal was able to see causes of events and foresee consequences more clearly than others. This seeing into history made him gallop into action which his own contemporaries could not appreciate or comprehend. Since he was earnest about what he perceived to be the trend of events, he expressed his views openly, but when his warnings went unheeded he grew impatient. For example, he saw in 1922 that the only honorable course open for India was complete independence, political and economic; and he earnestly hoped and appealed to the Congress to make the achievement of complete independence as its goal. At that time congressmen thought that that was a schoolboy's attitude. Five years later when he moved the famous Independence Resolution at the Madras session of the Congress in December 1927, that was considered an "academic" resolution, moved by a rash and unrealistic newcomer.[5] It was only in 1936 that the Congress took seriously the question of complete independence and gave up some of the illusions it had about the British promised home-rule and dominion status which in effect were never granted. Yet when Jawaharlal was ignored, and the Congress under Gandhi's leadership compromised on the goal of complete independence, Jawaharlal disagreed publicly with everyone, including his father and Gandhi, but he did not break with the Congress. His earnestness did not blind him to the reality that only those who climb the mountains see the dawn earlier, and others will come to behold it eventually.

Jawaharlal's earnestness about the social, economic and political changes in the human societies in the world was not that of an uncompromising reformer who would be martyred, but of a humanistic politician who distinguished a principle from a policy and saw the duty of men engaged in public affairs. Thus Jawaharlal's humanism essentially remaining on this side of the existentialists, was devoid of the dogma, superstitions, or doctrinaire approach, and was marked by the spirit of scientific rationalism which he identified with the Upanishadic spirit of inquiry, of seeking to rationalize every department of human activity from physics to public affairs, not excluding religion.

In his earnestness to secure for the Indian people (and for that matter, for people fighting for freedom everywhere), the essential freedoms and a better way of life, Jawaharlal considered many formulas and prescriptions devised by men in different conditions. While those ideologies for human development, no doubt, had some element of good in them, he recognized they all had the limitations of their particular situations, and the malady of their excess. Whether it was capitalism or communism, socialism or kibbutzuism, or sarvodaya, in his earnestness to change the existing conditions of the people, Jawaharlal felt that the bipolarization of these ideologies (as if they were dualistic religious dogmas) was unnecessary, since those ideologies could only be means to an end and not ends in themselves. Thus Jawaharlal's attitude to social justice and restructuring of societies towards that goal, was clearly marked by a nondogmatic, nonpartisan, noncommitted, nondoctrinaire approach to life and its varying possibilities, while his critics wanted him to adhere or stick to or identify with one particular exclusive current ideology or creed:

> But words and labels confuse. What I seek is an elimination of the profit motive in society and its replacement by a spirit of social service, cooperation taking the place of competition, production for consumption instead of for profit. Because I hate violence and consider it an abomination I cannot tolerate willingly our present system which is based on violence. I seek, therefore, an enduring and peaceful system from which the roots of violence have been removed, and where hatred shrivels up and yields place to nobler feelings. All this I call socialism.[6]

Throughout his writings, one could see this thread of social justice. Whether it was justice for the Ethiopians or the Czechoslovakians, Arabs or Jews, Chinese or Japanese, Britons or Indians, Jawaharlal's prime concern remained essentially with the people and not the few individuals who had institutionalized their greed or excessive ambitions and camouflaged their conceits, seeking domination over other peoples. Socialism for him meant an ideal society, working on humane principles, achieved through a variety of means.

IV *Conversational Style*

Jawaharlal's art of writing is not one of a cultivated craftsman or of one who has been perfecting his way of writing in a second language. His works exhibit an easy-flowing, personal, conversational style. Because of this directness, even the dry historical material becomes enlivened in his writings and easily readable.

"I am a lover of words" Jawaharlal had declared in the court at his own trial, "and try to use them appropriately." This appropriateness of words to fit thoughts and feelings comes from Jawaharlal's buoyant personality wanting to communicate with the masses who taught him the art of conversation without the sophistication of a chiseler of words or perfecter of language. The immediacy of action and the urgency of the situation perhaps left him no choice for revision or ornamentation.

Because of the directness of his statements it seems Jawaharlal is almost often speaking rather than writing. Whether it is a statement, or a letter, or a survey of historical period, or an account of travel, his writings have the flavor of a close dialogue. There is no studied rhetoric in his political writings, or academic jargon in his historical narratives, nor the trite criticalness in his various essays and articles. Though some of his writings repeat his ideas, there is hardly any excess in words. This measured appropriateness in the writings of a lover of words perhaps comes from the sincerity of the man and the straightforward manner in which he expresses his convictions and opinions.

V Contribution to Modern Indian Literature

Modern Indian literature being a composite and multi-foliate expression, is produced in seventeen officially recognized languages, namely, four Dravidian languages (Kannada, Malayalam, Tamil, and Telugu), ten Sanskrit derived languages (Assamese, Bengali, and Oriya in the east; Marathi, Gujarathi, and Sindhi in the west; Panjabi and Kashmiri in the north; Hindi and Maithili in the center), one all-India language (Sanskrit), and two leftover languages as imperial legacies by the Moghul and the British (Urdu and English). Though literatures in Urdu and English are late arrivals, Indian writers using these two languages have emerged from earlier imitative and timid works into more vigorous and artistic expression.

Indo-English literature began to emerge in India with the works of revolutionary Raja Rammohun Roy in the beginning of the nineteenth century. Towards the end of that century there were a number of poets writing verse; there were also some attempts at biography and fiction, and translations from Indian classics. In the twentieth century Indo-English literature achieved some distinction in fiction. English translation of Rabindranath Tagore's Bengali works gave a further impetus to this literature. A number of biographies and autobiographies were published but none of the persons portrayed therein was outstanding enough nor the writers had the creative gift to give their works artistic merits. The publication of the English translation of Mahatma Gandhi's autobiography in Gujarati, entitled *The Story of My Experiments in Truth* in 1936 was at once hailed as a classic in the simplest English prose. Though Gandhi originally wrote in Gujarati, the translation was made by his secretary Mahadev Desai under Gandhi's supervision, and the text clearly bears the imprint of Gandhi's unadorned personality.

Jawaharlal wrote all his works in English. He not only gave vitality to Indo-English literature, but also variety and originality. In his major works, the letters to his daughter, his autobiography, and his search for identity, Jawaharlal contributed three outstanding works to modern Indian Literature. Besides, his essays and articles, his delightful and charming travel accounts, and his uniquely original literary criticisms distinguish him as a man of letters of modern India.

VI *World Author*

The greatness of an author has to be judged by this impact on world culture and the pervasiveness of his thoughts and ideas. Time helps to determine outstanding authors of the past writers. Jawaharlal is still too near our time and no final judgment can be made about his work and his place among world authors.

Yet one cannot help recognizing the impact Jawaharlal made not only on modern India but on the world scene during his lifetime, both as a freedom fighter and later as the Prime Minister and world statesman. As a champion of the independent international policy of nonalignment he was interested in extending the area of peace and limiting the imperialistic alignments. In spite of its negative name, that policy had positive vitality inasmuch as it restrained the split of nations of the world into two alignments; instead, it generated a third alternative for developing nations by which they could assimilate the progress and methods of developed nations without being tied to their military and adventuristic pacts, commitments and groupings. In the pursuit of this policy, Jawaharlal's idealistic internationalism, humanistic socialism, commitment to freedom and democracy, reaffirm the essential human virtues, aspirations, and visions. The process of crystallization of these attitudes is to be found in his earlier writings. In that sense Jawaharlal's works are a key to his later-day policy as a world statesman. In them are the seeds of his thought, the designs of his vision and the rhythm of his humanistic attitudes. In his re-examination of history he re-echoes the perennial whisperings of the human spirit. During the long freedom struggle when he gave expression to his thoughts and ideas, his hopes, fears, tears and joy, he not only recognized a historical movement, but also consciously felt that he was acting on the world stage. It was by searching the past and examining the present, that he felt adventuring in the imprisoned cell of his being, and a record of that struggle and search for identity, including glimpses of truth, is of abiding interest to all the peoples of the world. Perhaps Jawaharlal Nehru may survive longer in the memory of mankind as an author than as a politician.

Notes and References

All page references to Jawaharlal Nehru's works in this study are to the following editions, indicated by capital letters:

AB   *An Autobiography*. London: The Bodley Head, 1953. New edition containing a supplementary chapter, "Five Years Later."

CSW   *China, Spain, and the War*. Allahabad: Kitabistan, 1940.

DI   *The Discovery of India*. Calcutta: The Signet Press, 1946.

EMI   *Eighteen Months in India, 1936–1937*. Allahabad: Kitabistan, 1938.

GWH   *Glimpses of World History*. With 50 maps by J. F. Horrabin. London: Lindsay Drummond Ltd., 1939. Rev. and up-to-date edition in one volume.

IW   *India and the World*. Ed. H. G. A. [Alexander]. London: George Allen & Unwin Ltd., 1936.

LFD   *Letters from Father to His Daughter*. Allahabad: Kitabistan, 1937. Fourth Impression.

REW   *Recent Essays and Writings*. Allahabad: Kitabistan, 1934.

SR   *Soviet Russia*. Allahabad: Kitabistan, 1928.

SSW   *Pandit Jawaharlal Nehru: Statements, Speeches, and Writings, 1922–1929*. Ed. L. Ram Mohan Lal. Allahabad: University and National Book Supplies, 1929.

TF   *Toward Freedom: The Autobiography of Jawaharlal Nehru*. Boston: Beacon Press, 1958.

UI   *The Unity of India, Collected Writings, 1937–1940*. Ed. V. K. Krishna Menon. London: Lindsay Drummond Ltd., 1942. Second Edition.

Chapter One

1. AB, p. 5.
2. *Ibid.*, p. 16.
3. *Ibid.*, p. 14.
4. *Ibid.*, p. 16.
5. *Ibid.*, p. 18.

6. *Ibid.*, p. 19.
7. *Ibid.*, pp. 21–22.
8. *Ibid.*, p. 21.
9. *Ibid.*, p. 20.
10. *Ibid.*, p. 26.
11. *Ibid.*, p. 23.
12. R.C. Majumdar et al., *An Advanced History of India* (London: Macmillan & Co., 1950), p. 984.
13. AB, p. 44.
14. *Ibid.*, p. 52.
15. *Ibid.*, p. 57.
16. *Ibid.*, p. 83.
17. *Ibid.*
18. *Ibid.*, p. 84.
19. *Ibid.*, p. 90.
20. *Ibid.*, p. 93.
21. *Ibid.*, p. 95.
22. *Ibid.*, p. 147.
23. SSW, pp. 93–95.
24. AB, p. 167.
25. SSW, pp. 114–27.

Chapter Two

1. SSW, preface.
2. See AB, ch. 21, pp. 148–55, for an account of Indian exiles in Europe.
3. *Nehru in Scandinavia* (Stockholm: Information Service of India, 1958), p. 116. Statements made during his goodwill visit to Denmark, Finland, Norway and Sweden in June 1957.

Chapter Three

1. SR, p. 3.
2. Also see AB, ch. 23, pp. 164–65.
3. See also Krishna Nehru Hutheesing, *With No Regrets* (New York: John Day Co., 1945), pp. 53–58.
4. Krishna Nehru Hutheesing with Alden Hatch, *We Nehrus* (New York: Holt, Rinehart and Winston, 1967), pp. 72–74.

Chapter Four

1. LFD, p. ix.
2. *Dhammapada*, chapter I, verse 1.

Chapter Five

1. GWH, p. 5.
2. Saul K. Padover, ed., *Nehru on World History* (New York: John Day & Co., 1960) p. xiii.
3. Letter 1, "A New Year's Gift"; 2, "The Lesson of History"; 3, "Inquilab Zindabad"; 19, "Three Months"; 20, "The Arabian Sea"; 21, "A Holiday and a Dream Journey"; 120, "Another New Year's Day"; and 196, "The Last Letter."
4. According to Indian Samvat era, Indira's birthday was observed on Oct. 26, though according to the Gregorian calendar it falls on Nov. 19.
5. Rabindranath Tagore, *Gitanjali* (London: Macmillan, 1913), Song 35.
6. Jawaharlal Nehru, "The Rashtrapati by Chanakya," in *The Modern Review* (Calcutta, Nov. 1937). Reproduced in TF, pp. i–iv.
7. The classical Indian schools of philosophy are regarded as *darsanas* or visionary perceptions of the truth; there are six such systems called Shaddarsanas, namely, Nyaya, Vaisesika, Samkhya, Yoga, Purva-Mimansa, and Uttara-Mimansa, or Vedanta.

Chapter Six

1. Ram Gopal, *The Trials of Nehru* (Bombay: The Book Center Private Ltd., 1962), Seventh Trial, pp. 72–80.
2. *Ibid.*, p. 78.
3. *Ibid.*, p. 80.
4. EMI, p. 17.
5. EMI, pp. 17–18.
6. EMI, p. 20.
7. See AB, 14–15.
8. Cf., AB, pp. 148–55.
9. DI, ch. 2, pp. 29–40.

Chapter Seven

1. See EMI, pp. 81–82.
2. Sir Frederick Whyte, *The Future of East and West* (London: Sidgwick, 1932). Quoted in UI, p. 15.
3. The absurdity of the archaic two-nation theory was grimly illustrated by the events leading to the massacre of Muslim Bengalis of former East Pakistan by the Muslim Army of West Pakistan in 1971, and the subsequent independence of Bangladesh. On the other hand Muslim mystics like Rumi have asserted the Upanishadic point of comparative religions, and in recent times Dr. Rafiq Zakaria has sought to demonstrate the secularism of Islam as taught by Prophet Mohammed in the Koran and the subsequent distortion of

those teachings by Muslim political and military adventurists. See Rafiq Zakaria, "Is Islam Secular?" in *The Illustrated Weekly of India* (Bombay, Oct. 28, 1974), pp. 6–19.

Chapter Eight

1. Carl Gustav Jung, "Psychology and Literature," from *Modern Man in Search of a Soul*, quoted in *The Creative Process*, ed. Brewster Ghiselin (Berkeley: University of California Press, 1952). Paperback edition, NAL/Mentor, p. 222.

2. Wu Cheng-en, *Hsi Yu Ki*, tr. Arthur Waley as *Monkey* (New York: Grove Press), p. 287.

Chapter Nine

1. GWH, p. 953.
2. DI, p. 26.
3. EMI, p. 17.
4. LFD, ch. 10, "What is Civilization?" pp. 35–36.
5. AB, p. 167.
6. EMI, p. 14.

Selected Bibliography

PRIMARY SOURCES

I Books

Soviet Russia: Some Random Sketches and Impressions. Ed. K. P. Dar., Allahabad: Allahabad Law Journal Press, 1928.

Pandit Jawaharlal Nehru: Statements, Speeches, and Writings. Ed. L. Ram Mohan Lal, with an appreciation by M. K. Gandhi. Allahabad: University and National Book Supplies, 1929.

Letters from a Father to His Daughter: Being a Brief Account of the Early Days of the World, Written for Children. Allahabad: Kitabistan, 1930.

Recent Essays and Writings: On the Future of India, Communalism, and Other Subjects. Allahabad: Kitabistan, 1934.

Glimpses of World History: Being Further Letters to His Daughter Written in Prison, and Containing a Rambling Account of History for Young People. 2 Vols. Allahabad: Kitabistan, 1934. Revised and up-to-date edition with a postscript and 50 maps by J. F. Horrabin. Allahabad: Kitabistan, 1939. Also London: Lindsay Drummond Ltd., 1939.

An Autobiography: With Musings on Recent Events in India. London: John Lane, The Bodley Head, 1936. Reprinted with an additional chapter "Five Years Later," appendices, 1942.
Republished under the title, *Toward Freedom: The Autobiography of Jawaharlal Nehru*, edited and abridged. New York: John Day Co., 1941. Reprinted in paperback with an introductory article "The Rastrapati" by Chanakya (pseud. of J. Nehru), epilogue, "The Parting of Ways," and appendices. Boston: Beacon Press, 1958.

India and the World: Essays. Ed. H. G. A. [Alexander]. London: George Allen & Unwin Ltd., 1936.

Eighteen Months in India, 1936–1937: Being Further Essays and Writings. Allahabad: Kitabistan, 1938.

China, Spain, and the War. Allahabad: Kitabistan, 1940.

The Unity of India: Collected Writings, 1937–1940. Edited with a foreword by V. K. Krishna Menon. London: Lindsay Drummond Ltd., 1941.

151

The Discovery of India. Calcutta: The Signet Press, 1946. Abridged edition with an introduction by Robert I. Crane, New York: Doubleday Co. Inc.. Anchor paperback edition, 1959.

II   Pamphlets

Whither India? Allahabad: Kitabistan, 1933.
A Window in Prison and Prison-Land. Allahabad: Kitabistan, 1933.
Spain: Why? London: Indian Committee for Food for Spain, 1937.
The Question of Language. Allahabad: Indian National Congress, 1937.
Where are We? Allahabad: Kitabistan, 1939. Articles 1–8, published in the *National Herald*, Lucknow, Feb./March, 1939, as *From Lucknow to Tripuri: A Survey of Congress Politics, 1936–1939*.
Jawaharlal Nehru on the Cripps Mission. London: India League, 1942.
India's Day of Reckoning. London: India League, 1942. Reprinted from *Fortune Magazine*, April 1942.
An Authoritative Statement on the Breakdown of the New Delhi Negotiations. London: India League, 1942.
India, What Next? Why the Talks Failed. London: India League, 1942. Jawaharlal Nehru and Abul Kalam Azad answer Sir Stafford Cripps, et. al.
Can Indians Get Together? New York: India League of America, 1942. Reprinted from *The New York Times*, July 19, 1942.
What India Wants. London: India League, 1942. Reprinted from *Fortune Magazine*, 1942.
Letter to African Leaders. Washington, D.C.: Indian Information Service, Oct. 15, 1946.
Prison Humors. Allahabad: New Literature, 1946.
Sri Ramakrishna and Swami Vivekananda. Mayavati, Almora: Advaita Ashram, 1949.
Towards a Socialist Order. New Delhi: Indian National Congress, 1955.
Towards a New Revolution. New Delhi: Indian National Congress, 1956.

III   Articles (Other than those articles included in books and pamphlets)

"Rashtrapathi." by Chanakya (pseud. of J. Nehru). *The Modern Review*. Calcutta, Nov. 1937. TF, 1958.
"Letter to a Young Chinese Journalist." *Life Magazine*. New York, Aug. 8, 1942.
"India can Learn from China." *Asia and the Americans*. January, 1943.
"India Speaks to China." *Life Magazine*. New York, March 1, 1943.
"Colonialism Must Go." *The New York Times Magazine*. March 3, 1946.
"A Cable from Pandit Nehru." *The New Republic*. New York, Aug. 4, 1947.
"Tagore and Gandhi." *Visva-Bharati*. Santiniketana. Gandhi Memorial Peace Number, 1949.

"Sri Ramkrishna, As I understand Him." *Vedanta for Modern Man.* Ed. Christopher Isherwood. New York: Harper & Bros., 1951.
"Changing India," *Foreign Affairs.* New York, April, 1963. Vol. XLI, No. 3.

IV   Prefaces to Books

Introduction, *Gandhiji: His Life and Work,* ed. D. G. Tendulkar *et al.* Bombay: the editor, 1945. Published on Gandhi's 75th birthday, October 2, 1944.
Introduction, *Kashmir, Eden of East* by S. N. Dhar. Allahabad: Kitab Mahal, 1945.
Foreword, *White Sahibs in India* by Arthur Reynold. London: The Socialist Book Center, Ltd., 1946.
Foreword, *To a Gandhian Capitalist,* ed. Kaka Kalelkar. Wardha: The Jamnalal Seva Trust, 1951. Correspondence between Mahatma Gandhi and Jamnalal Bajaj and members of his family.
Foreword, *Mahatma: Life of Mohandas Karamchand Gandhi* by D. G. Tendulkar. Bombay: Vithalbhai K. Jhaveri and D. G. Tendulkar, 1951–1954.
Introudction, *Indian Temple Sculpture* by K. M. Munshi. Calcutta: A. Goswami, 1956.
Foreword, *A Philosophy for NEFA,* ed. Sachin Roy. Shillong: North East Frontier Agency, 1959.

V   Letters

Nehru-Jinnah Correspondence. Allahabad: J. B. Kripalani, General-Secretary, All-India Congress Committee, 1938. Including Gandhi-Jinnah, and Nehru-Nawab Ismail Correspondence.
A Bunch of Old Letters. Bombay: Asia Publishing House, 1958. Written mostly to Jawaharlal Nehru, and some written by him.
Nehru's Letters to His Sister, ed. with Introduction by Krishna Nehru Hutheesing. London: Faber and Faber, 1963.
Letters from Gandhi, Nehru, Vinoba. Leiden: E. J. Brill, 1968.

VI   Speeches and Conferences

A. Collections

Before and After Independence. Ed. J. S. Bright. New Dehli: Indian Printing Works, 1950. A collection of the most important speeches, 1922–1950.
Jawaharlal Nehru: Independence and After: A Collection of Speeches, 1946–1949. Vol. I. New Delhi: Government of India, Ministry of Information, Publications Division, 1949.
Jawaharlal Nehru's Speeches, 1949–1953. Vol. II. New Delhi: Government of India, Ministry of Information, Publications Division, 1954.

Jawaharlal Nehru's Speeches, 1953–1957. Vol. III. New Delhi: Government of India, Ministry of Information, Publications Division, 1958.

India's Foreign Policy New Delhi: Government of India, Ministry of Information, Publications Division, 1961.

Jawaharlal Nehru's Speeches, 1957–1963. Vol. IV. New Delhi: Government of India, Ministry of Information, Publications Division, 1964.

Jawaharlal Nehru's Speeches, 1963–1964. Vol. V. New Delhi: Government of India, Ministry of Information, Publications Division, 1965.

B. Conferences

Talks with Nehru, ed. Norman Cousins. New York: John Day, 1951.

Press Conferences. New Delhi: Information Service of India, 1953.

Press Conferences. New Delhi: Information Service of India, 1955.

Conversations with Mr. Nehru, ed. Tibor Mende. London: Secker & Warburg, 1956.

Kashmir and Indo-Pakistan Relations. Interview by Michael Brecher. New Delhi: Information Service of India, 1956.

The Mind of Mr. Nehru. As revealed in a series of intimate talks with R. K. Karanjia. London: George Allen & Unwin Ltd., 1960.

VII   Selections from Writings and Speeches

Mahatma Gandhi. Calcutta: The Signet Press, 1949.

Selected Writings of J. Nehru, 1916–1950. Ed. J. S. Bright. New Delhi: The Indian Printing Works, 1950.

Selections from Jawaharlal Nehru. Ed. S. K. Narain. London: Oxford University Press, 1956.

India's Spokesman. Ed. C. D. Narasimhaiah. Madras & London: Macmillan & Co., 1960.

Wit and Wisdom of Jawaharlal Nehru. Ed. N. B. Sen. New Delhi: New Book Society of India, 1960.

The Quintessence of Nehru. Ed. K. T. Narasimha Char. London: George Allen & Unwin Ltd., 1961.

Glorious Thoughts of Nehru. Ed. N. B. Sen. New Delhi: New Book Society of India, 1964.

Nehru: The First Sixty Years. Ed. Dorothy Norman. 2 Vols. New York: John Day Co., 1965. Vol. I: Beginning to 1939; Vol. II: 1940–1950.

SECONDARY SOURCES

AHUJA, B. N. *Jawaharlal Nehru: The Leader of East and West*. Lahore: Varma Publishing Co., 1947.

APSLER, ALFRED. *Fighter for Independence, Jawaharlal Nehru*. New York: J. Messener, 1963.

BAWA, T. *Nehru's India. An analytical study.* New Delhi: Freeland Publications Private Ltd., 1956.

BOSE, SUBHAS CHANDRA. *The Indian Struggle.* Calcutta: Thacker, Spink Co., 1948.

BOWLES, CHESTER. *Ambassador's Report.* New York: Harper & Bros. 1954.

BRECHER, MICHAEL. *Nehru: A Political Biography.* London & New York: Oxford University Press, 1959. Abridged paperback edition, Boston: Beacon Press, 1962. An objective historical account of Jawaharlal's political career, readable and comprehensive.

BRIGHT, J. S. *The Life of Jawaharlal Nehru.* New Delhi: Indian Printing Works, 1958. Also: Lahore: Indian Printing Works, 1946.

————. *Will Nehru Survive His Greatness?* New Delhi: Indian Printing Works, 1950.

CAMPBELL-JOHNSON, ALAN. *Mission with Mountbatten.* London: Robert Hale, 1951.

CHAKRABARTI, ATULANANDA. *Nehru: His Democracy and India.* Calcutta: Thackers Press, 1961. Critically examines democracy in ancient India, and Jawaharlal's attempts to assimilate European socialistic and democratic ideals.

CHHIBBER, V. N. *Jawaharlal Nehru: A Man of Letters.* Delhi: Vikas Publications, 1970. Sketchy accounts of occasional writings, and some analysis of major works.

CROCKER, WALTER RUSSEL. *Nehru, a Contemporary's Estimate.* Foreword by Arnold Toynbee. New York: Oxford University Press, 1966.

DASA, MANMATHA NATHA. *The Political Philosophy of Jawaharlal Nehru.* New York: John Day, 1961. London: G. Allen & Unwin Ltd., 1961.

EDWARDES, MICHAEL. *Nehru: A Pictorial Biography.* London: Thames & Hudson, 1962. New York: Viking Press, 1962.

GOEL, SITA RAM. *In Defence of Comrade Krishna Menon: A Political Biography of Pandit Nehru.* New Delhi: Bharati Sahitya Sadan, 1963. A bitter attack on Jawaharlal's socialistic policies by the spokesman of anticommunist front.

GOPAL, RAM. *The Trials of Nehru.* Bombay: The Book Center Private Ltd., 1962. Gives details of nine political trials and imprisonments of Jawaharlal.

GUNTHER, JOHN. *Inside Asia.* New York: Harper Brothers, 1939.

GUTHRIE, ANN. *Madame Ambassador:* The Life of Vijaya Laksmi Pandit. New York: Harcourt Brace & World, 1962.

HUSAIN, SYED ABID. *The Way of Gandhi and Nehru.* Bombay: Asia Publishing House, 1959.

HUTHEESING, KRISHNA NEHRU. *With No Regrets.* Bombay: Padma Publications, 1944. Intimate chronical of family life.

————. *We Nehrus.* New York: Holt, Rinehart and Winston, 1967. Personal account of an important political family, depicting many family scenes.

JOLLY, G. S. ed. *The Image of Nehru*. Delhi: Prabhu Book Service, 1968. Contains fifteen articles by eminent men, contributed as a homage on the fourth anniversary of Jawaharlal's death.

KARAKA, DOSABHAI FRAMJI. *Nehru: The Lotus Eater from Kashmir*. London: Derek Verschoyla, 1953. Attempts to demonstrate failure of Jawaharlal as a prime minister because of the "unbridgeable gulf between his theory and practice."

KRIPALANI, KRISHNA R. *Gandhi, Tagore, and Nehru*. Bombay: Hind Kitabs, 1949.

KRISHNAMURTI, Y. G. *Jawaharlal Nehru: The Man and his Idea*. Bombay: Popular Book Depot, 1942.

LAMB, BEATRICE PITNEY. *The Nehrus of India*: Three Generations of Leadership. New York: Macmillan Co., 1967.

MALAVIYA, K. D. *Motilal Nehru: His Life and Speeches*. Allahabad: Kitabistan, 1919.

MASANI, SAKUNTALA. *Nehru Story*. New York: Oxford University Press, 1949.

MOHAN, ANAND. *Indira Gandhi, A Personal and Political Biography*. New York: Meredith Press, 1968.

MORAES, FRANK [FRANCIS ROBERT]. *Jawaharlal Nehru: A Biography*. New York: The Macmillan Co., 1956. Primarily a political biography against the background of Indian nationalist movement; informative and readable.

NANDA, BAL RAM. *The Nehrus: Motilal and Jawaharlal*. London: George Allen & Unwin Ltd., 1962.

NARASIMHAIAH, C. D. *Jawaharlal Nehru: A Study of His Writings and Speeches*. Mysore: Rao and Raghavan, 1960. Discusses literary qualities of major books and speeches.

NEHRU: *Nehru Abhinandan Granth*. Delhi: Nehru Abhinandan Granth Committee, 1949. A Volume presented to the Prime Minister on his sixtieth birthday, Nov. 14, 1949, containing sixty-one articles and eighteen anecdotes.

PANDIT, VIJAYA LAKSHMI. *So I Became a Minister*. Allahabad: Kitabistan, 1939.

———. *Prison Days*. Allahabad: Kitabistan, 1946.

PATEL, BABURAO. *Burning Words*. Bombay: Sumati Publications, 1957. A critical history of nine years of Jawaharlal's rule from 1947 to 1956.

PHIBBS, PHILIP M. *Nehru's Philosophy of International Relations*. Chicago University Library, 1957. Microfilm 5460 DS.

RANGE, WILLARD. *Jawaharlal Nehru's World View*. Athens: University of Georgia Press, 1961. Discusses Jawaharlal's theory of international relations.

SAHGAL, NAYANTARA. *Prison and Chocolate Cake*. New York: Alfred A. Knopf, 1954.

SITARAMAYYA, PATTABHI. *History of Indian National Congress*. 2 Vols. Bombay: Indian National Congress, 1935 and 1947.

SETON, MARIE. *Panditji: A Portrait of Jawaharlal Nehru*. London: Dobson 1967.

SHARMA, JAGADISH SARAN. *Jawaharlal Nehru: A Descriptive Bibliography*. Delhi: S. Chand & Co., 1955.

SHEEAN, JAMES VINCENT. *Nehru: The Years of Power*. New York: Random House, 1960.

SINGH, ANUP. *Nehru: The Rising Star of India*. London: George Allen & Unwin Ltd., 1940.

SMITH, DONALD EUGENE. *Nehru and Democracy*. Bombay: Orient Longmans, 1958. Analyzes the political thoughts of an Asian democrat.

TANDON, P. D. *The Human Nehru*. Allahabad: Allahabad Law Journal Press, 1957.

UNESCO, *Nehru and the Modern World*. New Delhi: Indian National Commission for UNESCO, 1968. Papers read at a conference, "Jawaharlal Nehru's Role in Modern World," Sept. 26, 1966, in New Delhi.

VENKATESWARAN, R. J. *The Impact of Jawaharlal Nehru on Indian Economy*. Calcutta: Oxford Book Co., 1962.

ZAKARIA, RAFIQ, ed. *A Study of Nehru*. Bombay: The Times of India Press, 1959. Issued on Jawaharlal's seventieth birthday, containing various aspects of his personality, viewed by sixty-two international contributors; includes a detailed chronology, and a survey in pictures.

Index

159